VIRGINIA SUMMITS

Help Us Keep This Guide Up to Date

Every effort has been made by the author and editors to make this guide as accurate and useful as possible. However, many things can change after a guide is published—trails are rerouted, regulations change, techniques evolve, facilities come under new management, etc.

We appreciate hearing from you concerning your experiences with this guide and how you feel it could be improved and kept up to date. While we may not be able to respond to all comments and suggestions, we'll take them to heart and we'll also make certain to share them with the author. Please send your comments and suggestions to falconeditorial@rowman.com.

Thanks for your input, and happy trails!

VIRGINIA SUMMITS

40 BEST MOUNTAIN HIKES FROM THE
SHENANDOAH VALLEY TO SOUTHWEST VIRGINIA

Erin Gifford

FALCONGUIDES

ESSEX, CONNECTICUT

For Dirk, Clare, Max, Molly, and Paul

FALCONGUIDES®

An imprint of Globe Pequot, the trade division of
The Rowman & Littlefield Publishing Group, Inc.
4501 Forbes Blvd., Ste. 200
Lanham, MD 20706
www.rowman.com

Falcon and FalconGuides are registered trademarks and Make Adventure Your Story is a
trademark of The Rowman & Littlefield Publishing Group, Inc.

Distributed by NATIONAL BOOK NETWORK

Photos by Erin Gifford unless otherwise noted
Maps by Melissa Baker and The Rowman & Littlefield Publishing Group, Inc.

British Library Cataloguing in Publication Information available

Library of Congress Cataloging-in-Publication Data
Names: Gifford, Erin, 1973– author.
Title: Virginia summits : 40 best mountain hikes from the Shenandoah Valley to Southwest
Virginia / Erin Gifford.
Description: Essex, Connecticut : Falcon Guides, [2023]
Identifiers: LCCN 2022046165 (print) | LCCN 2022046166 (ebook) | ISBN 9781493069491
(paperback) | ISBN 9781493069507 (epub)
Subjects: LCSH: Hiking—Virginia—Guidebooks. | Trails—Virginia—Guidebooks. | Virginia—
Guidebooks.
Classification: LCC GV199.42.V8 G54 2023 (print) | LCC GV199.42.V8 (ebook) | DDC
796.5109755—dc23/eng/20221013
LC record available at https://lccn.loc.gov/2022046165
LC ebook record available at https://lccn.loc.gov/2022046166

♾️™ The paper used in this publication meets the minimum requirements of American National
Standard for Information Sciences—Permanence of Paper for Printed Library Materials, ANSI/
NISO Z39.48-1992.

The author and The Rowman & Littlefield Publishing Group, Inc. assume no liability for accidents
happening to, or injuries sustained by, readers who engage in the activities described in this
book.

CONTENTS

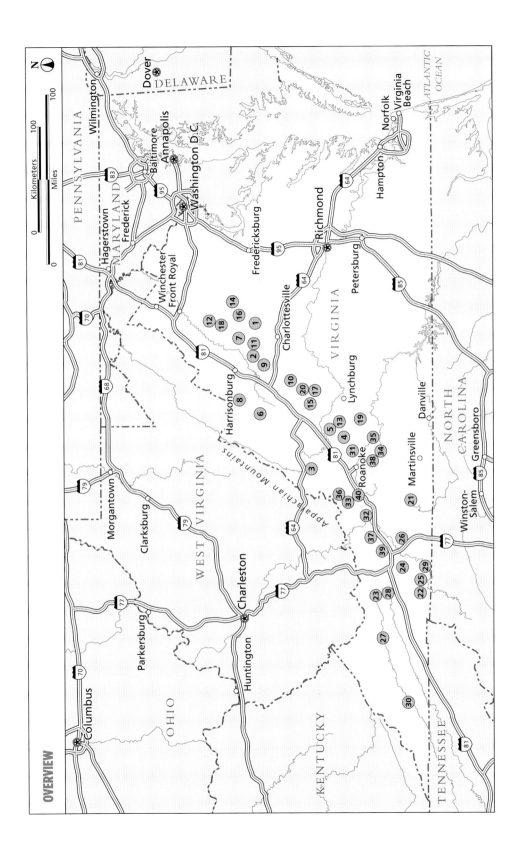

OVERVIEW

ACKNOWLEDGMENTS

I want to thank my husband, Dirk. I am grateful for your unwavering support and help with the kids as I crisscrossed Virginia to evaluate hikes for this book. To our kids, Clare, Max, Molly, and Paul, thank you for keeping your grades up and helping Dad make dinner while I was on the trails.

A big thank-you to my editor, Mason Gadd with FalconGuides, for seeing this guidebook to completion. I still can't believe this is my third book with FalconGuides. It's been an adventure for which I am so incredibly grateful.

To Ann Payes, the best-ever hiking partner. I cherish all the photos I have of you up ahead on the hiking trail, and appreciate that you are a quick study. Yes, I'm taking another photo. Yes, you can keep moving because I want an action shot on the trail. Also, you are still and will always be witty. To Matt Payes, I will always accept your on-point roast beef sandwiches. Keep 'em coming.

Thank you to the hiker friends I've made on the trails, including Jacqueline Poore Holzman (aka RVA Hiker Girl) and Jessica Bowser, podcaster extraordinaire with the Virginia Outdoor Adventures Podcast, as well as to those I met along the way on MeetUp hikes, like Pam, Doris, Claudine, and Patty. One final shout-out to my parents, in-laws, friends, and siblings—thank you for your love and support.

MEET YOUR GUIDE

Erin Gifford has been writing about travel and outdoor recreation for more than fifteen years. She has written magazine, newspaper, and online articles for such media outlets as the *Washington Post*, *Chicago Tribune*, *Family Circle*, *Parents*, CNN.com, *Health*, *Northern Virginia Magazine*, AFAR.com, and *AAA World*. She is the founder of GoHikeVirginia .com, a website she created in April 2020 to introduce fellow outdoor lovers to the hiking trails of Virginia. In her spare time, Erin enjoys family road trips, exploring national parks, running half-marathons, and, of course, hiking. She is currently working toward completing a half-marathon in every US state. She lives in northern Virginia with her husband, four children, and one quirky dog.

High Knob Tower View

INTRODUCTION

For those who want to climb the highest mountains, this book's for you. At least if you're eager to tackle the peaks of Virginia. We've got some good ones, too. We may not have 14ers like in Colorado—you know, summits that top 14,000 feet—but we do have some mighty impressive mountains in the Old Dominion. Virginia is home to eight mountain ranges, including the Blue Ridge Mountains and Appalachian Mountains. Virginia also has five peaks that stand at more than 5,000 feet above sea level. The highest peak is Mount Rogers, a rugged 5,729-foot-tall mountain located at Mount Rogers National Recreation Area in Southwest Virginia.

Virginia's mountain ranges cut diagonally across the west side of the state, from the Shenandoah Valley all the way to the far southwest tip of the state that touches Tennessee and Kentucky. The 196,000-acre Shenandoah National Park has ninety-three named peaks, including Hawksbill Mountain, the tallest mountain in the park, which tops out at 4,050 feet. You'll also find the Appalachian Trail in Virginia. Nearly 550 miles of this iconic hiking trail meander across the state—up, over, and around scenic mountains, like The Priest in Tyro and Tinker Mountain in Catawba.

Rocky overlooks and outcrops are plentiful across the jagged mountains of Virginia, rewarding determined hikers with sensational panoramas as far as the eye can see. Some peaks are challenging to reach, requiring arduous treks and rock scrambles, but not all big views require big effort. Some summit hikes, like those ushering hikers to the top of High Knob near Harrisonburg and Buffalo Mountain near Floyd, are short, sweet, and satisfying.

The hikes in this guidebook run on the moderate to strenuous side, though you will find a sprinkling of easy summit hikes. The longest hike is nearly 15 miles, but most hikes are in the more manageable range of 4 to 6 miles. All hikes have been tested and have earned a spot in this guidebook for their well-maintained trails, delightful flora and fauna, and spectacular views that will leave you breathlessly ready to take on your next summit hike.

THE HIKING REGIONS

Virginia is a sizable state, so this guidebook is divided into three regions to help you pinpoint the location of each hike and, importantly, the driving distance from your location.

Shenandoah Valley. Shenandoah National Park is the most well-known and trafficked section of the 200-mile-long Shenandoah Valley, which is home to the lion's share of peak hikes in this book. Nine of these hikes are within the 105-mile-long stretch of Shenandoah National Park. These hikes feature jagged ridges, tumbling waterfalls, boulder scrambles, and flowing rivers. That's in addition to the far-reaching vistas that are part and parcel of a good summit hike. Several hikes boast 360-degree views. Get ready to feel on top of the world.

Southwest Virginia. This rugged section of Virginia is the least-explored region of the state, but it may also be the most beautiful thanks to its valleys, ridges, grassy balds, and highlands. The landscapes are mesmerizing, whether you're taking it all in from a high-elevation pond or a rocky outcrop that doles out views for miles and miles. Interestingly, the high peaks in Southwest Virginia have more to offer beyond, well, peak views. Ogle a curiously large sand cave on the way to White Rocks in Ewing, and a sandstone labyrinth of deep crevices atop Middle Knob near Saltville. Free-roaming wild ponies frequent the trails near the state's highpoint, Mount Rogers.

Virginia Mountains. This mountainous region is well known as a mecca for outdoor enthusiasts eager to hike, bike, and paddle, even fish and boat on the area's lakes, like Smith Mountain Lake, the state's second-largest lake. The Appalachian Trail and the Blue Ridge Parkway crisscross the southern section of the Virginia Mountains region. In the north, the Appalachian Mountains and George Washington and Jefferson National Forest captivate peak-bagging hikers of all levels. The area is home to two hiking trifectas that top many bucket lists, including Virginia's Triple Crown in Catawba (McAfee Knob, Tinker Cliffs, and Dragon's Tooth) and the Peaks of Otter in Bedford (Sharp Top, Flat Top, and Harkening Hill). All six trophy hikes brim with wildly inspiring views that will leave even the most avid hikers at a loss for words.

WEATHER

Virginia is a four-season state. Expect snow, rain, ice, warm sun, hot sun, lightning storms, and hailstorms. You can also expect plenty of clear blue-sky days. Virginia is not prone to extreme weather or weather events, such as avalanches, earthquakes, tornados, or hurricanes.

WINTER

Snowfall can vary wildly from year to year. However, more snow tends to fall in the mountains. You may not see a flake when you buckle up in the car, then find a snow-covered trail on arrival at the trailhead. Consider traction spikes, like Kahtoola MICROspikes, and hiking poles for stability and balance if you plan to hike in snow.

Some hikes are just not safe in winter or on snow or ice, like Old Rag and Bearfence Mountain. Rock scrambles become slick, unmanageable, and dangerous. That's not to say that these hikes are not good in winter. They can be wonderful in winter, when the air is crisp and the fair-weather hikers are bundled up at home. However, it's wise not to attempt hikes with rock scrambles when conditions are unsafe. Avoid a winter rescue on the hiking trail.

SPRING

Rain is a given in spring in Virginia. Toss waterproof pants and a jacket in your daypack if rain is in the forecast. Any day is a great day to get outside, even in the rain, which tends not to be especially cold. In spring, rain leads to gushing waterfalls. Several summit hikes in this book are worth saving for spring when water is more plentiful, like Three Ridges. This hike guides hikers alongside tumbling waterfalls nearly the entire way up the Mau-Har Trail.

Meantime, the rivers along the Bear Church Rock and Terrapin Mountain hikes can be dramatic when the water is really flowing after a solid rain. Take heed, as water crossings can become treacherous during and after a rainstorm. Some waterways can turn from gentle streams to raging rivers, so stay aware and make good choices. If water is deeper than your ankles, turn around and complete the hike another day. Some especially fierce water crossings have required emergency rescues.

SUMMER

Summer is a wonderful time to hike to high peaks, but it's also a time when everyone wants to get outdoors on the trails. The weather is nice, especially in early summer before it gets humid and steamy, and we all want to escape to the mountains. Temperatures can be ten degrees cooler in the mountains than in the valleys down below. Ah, refreshing.

Bugs are also a part of summer hiking. Mosquitoes, blackflies, ticks, and gnats are the most common (and hated) flying pests on the trails in Virginia. However, a good breeze at a mountain summit can often be enough to blow the bugs away. Slather or spray on insect repellent before you hit the trail. One to try is Sawyer's picaridin-based insect repellent, given its effectiveness as an alternative to DEET-based repellents.

Choose an EPA-approved insect repellent that is friendly to the environment. For extra protection, wear barrier clothing, like long sleeves, pants, and ankle gaiters. Wide-brim hats are good too and should be treated with a clothing treatment, like permethrin, before wearing.

Terrapin Mountain Waterfall

FALL

Virginia is known for striking fall colors, including leaves of amber, gold, and bronze. The 105-mile Skyline Drive that runs north to south along the length of Shenandoah National Park can get bumper-to-bumper busy in late fall, as can the winding Blue Ridge Parkway.

In fall the weather is rather mild. Typically, a light jacket or sweater is all you need to enjoy the beautiful weather and colorful foliage. Leaf peepers, note that peak fall colors occur earlier at higher elevations in the mountains.

Fall foliage season is easily the most popular time of year to be on the trails, especially at Shenandoah National Park. Parking lots fill up very early, and trails can become unbearably crowded, as can panoramic summits. If you can, get an early start or go on weekdays.

FLORA AND FAUNA

Virginia is home to a diverse array of plants and animals. Across the state it's not unusual to see such wildlife as black bears, white-tailed deer, red foxes, eastern cottontail rabbits, and yellow-bellied slider turtles. There are also bobcats, copperheads, and even rattlesnakes in Virginia.

There are two primary landscapes in Virginia, depending on which side of the fall line you are on. The fall line essentially runs north to south along I-95. On the west side, which is home to the state's peaks, you'll find largely deciduous forest with oak, maple, elm, and birch trees. You'll also find more than a few coniferous varieties, like white pines, red pines, and red spruce trees, particularly at higher elevations.

In the late spring, trillium and mountain laurel are abundant, especially in the western mountains. Bluebells that range in color from lilac to cobalt can be found at lower elevations in early to mid-spring. Flowering tulips, daffodils, crocuses, rhododendrons, and hyacinths are also native to Virginia and are easy to find blooming in spring.

FEES AND PERMITS

There is typically no fee to enter and hike in national forests, regional parks, and local parks in Virginia. However, entry into Shenandoah National Park, as well as parking at nearly all state parks, requires a fee year-round, even if there is no attending ranger at the entrance station.

For Shenandoah National Park, there are several fee options. Many visitors purchase an annual pass for entry for one calendar year. You can purchase an annual pass specific to Shenandoah National Park or an America the Beautiful pass that's good at all national park service units. Both can be purchased online or at the entrance station when you arrive at the park.

Almost every state park requires an entry fee, too. In the off-season, when there is no attendant, look for a yellow envelope to place cash into and deposit in the on-site repository. Before you do, tear off the receipt to place on your dashboard as proof of payment.

Note that several US Forest Service–managed units, including Cascades Day Use Area and Raccoon Branch Campground, also require a parking fee by way of cash payment in an envelope to deposit on-site. Both accept the annual national parks pass. If you have one, simply scribble your passholder number on the envelope and deposit in the repository.

Fees can change from year to year, so in this guidebook, we identify fees by way of a scale:

$ = $1–$5	$$$ = $16–$25
$$ = $6–$15	$$$$ = $25+

LEAVE NO TRACE PRINCIPLES

If you take away only one thing from this guidebook, we hope it will be the seven Leave No Trace principles. Being a first-time or newbie hiker is no excuse not to abide by any of these guiding principles in order to preserve and protect nature for current and future generations.

We've been on too many hikes where we've seen one or more of the following:

- Visitors getting way too close to—even stalking—wildlife in their natural habitat
- Trash left behind, including dirty diapers, fast-food containers, soda cans, and empty chip bags
- Initials carved into trees with pocketknives
- Stacks of rocks (i.e., rock cairns) not created by park rangers or trail stewards
- Destroying the tranquility of nature with loud noises, including music and words

Mary's Rock Summit Views

The ultimate goal of the Leave No Trace principles is to minimize human impact on the outdoors. Here is what you can do to reduce your footprint in the wild:

1. **Plan ahead and prepare.** Do not put yourself and others at risk by wearing improper footwear, not carrying enough water, wearing inappropriate clothing, and not adequately illuminating your hike (if setting off before sunrise or returning after sunset). Poor preparation can lead to resource damage, particularly when a rescue is required.

2. **Travel and camp on durable surfaces.** For the most part, this means stay on the trails. Do not go off trail to get close to a river, to visit with wildlife, or to reach an unmarked viewpoint. By staying on designated hiking trails, you reduce the creation of multiple routes that damage the landscape. Do not take shortcuts on switchback trails or camp on vegetation.

3. **Dispose of waste properly.** The forest is not your trash can or dumpster. If you pack it in, pack it out. That means leave with what you brought in, including single-use water bottles and snack wrappers, even toilet paper if you must squat in a hole outdoors. Do not bury anything that will not naturally decompose.

4. **Leave what you find.** Enjoy the sights on a hike, including wildflowers, tree leaves, mushrooms, and pine cones, but leave them be. Do not bring them home. Avoid harming live plants or trees (carving your initials on a tree is obviously a no-no). Unless specifically allowed and noted, do not bring home any natural or cultural objects as souvenirs.

5. **Minimize campfire impacts.** If you must build a fire, use a camping stove or a fire ring specifically created for campfires. Consider the severity of the fire danger for the time of year and location. Also, make certain that a fire is allowed, and contemplate the potential damage to the forested region. If you build a fire, know how to properly extinguish it.

6. **Respect wildlife.** Do not feed the bears, or any wildlife for that matter. Do not approach wild animals—whether mild-mannered deer or photo-worthy black bears. Observe all wildlife from a safe and respectful distance. Sudden movements and loud noises can cause wildlife undue stress. You are in their home. Stay back, and let them go about their daily lives.

7. **Be considerate of other visitors.** We all need to share the trails and respect fellow hikers. Do not play loud music, do not scream or make loud noises, and do not let your off-leash dog run way up the trail. Control your volume and your pet to allow everyone to be awed and inspired by the surrounding nature.

BEFORE YOU HIT THE TRAIL

There are many exquisite views to behold from the tops of mountains across Virginia. You may have trouble determining where to begin. We get it. Honestly, every summit vista in this book is so completely Instagram-worthy. Decisions, decisions. Thankfully, every hike in this guidebook will impress and inspire even your most critical followers. Translation: You can't go wrong with any hike in this book. Every single one is chock-full of photogenic landscapes and overlooks.

With this guide in hand—or at the very least, on your night table—you're prepared to shout, sing, maybe yodel, from more than a few mountaintops in Virginia. Every hike features directions to the trailhead, a topo map, color photos, and step-by-step directions once you reach the trailhead. Grab your daypack, fill your water bottle, and slather on sunblock—it's time for a hike.

As you read the hike descriptions, note that each one includes **distance** and **difficulty.** Nearly every hike in this book is moderate or strenuous. That's just the nature of a hike to a high peak. You've got to go up. Along the same lines, you'll find **maximum grade,** which essentially tells you the elevation of the trail. The higher the number, the steeper the hiking trail. You'll be hard-pressed to find many hikes with less than 25 percent, but even then, it's not for a long stretch. Rarely will you be on a long, unrelenting slog up a hill to the summit. As for distance, most hikes are 4 to 6 miles but can be as many as 15 miles. Hikes typically have an **elevation gain** of at least 500 feet over the course of the hike, though some can be close to 4,000 feet. All this means it's important that you bring lots of water and high-energy snacks to refuel on the way up and down.

The **hiking time** is how long a hike may take you from start to finish, including time spent savoring views or splashing in swimming holes. Your mileage may vary, of course. You may take more or less time. It's your hike. No need to rush. The hiking time is a rough baseline to give you a general idea of what to expect in terms of time spent on the hiking trail.

For **best seasons,** most hikes in this book are good year-round. Even a summit hike can be good in winter, but bring extra layers, because it can sometimes be surprisingly windy and cold at the top (often much colder than at the trailhead). Pay attention to hikes that list rock scrambles in the **trail surface** section. These hikes can become slick and treacherous when covered in rain, ice, and snow. Save these summit hikes for a precipitation-free day.

For **maps,** many of the trails can be found on a corresponding National Geographic Trails Illustrated topographic map for the region. You can also find nearly every trail and park listed in this guidebook online, too. This leads us to **cell service.** This is important, so important that every hike includes the strength of cell service—from nonexistent to

◀ House Mountain Table Rock

reliable (as evaluated on an AT&T iPhone). Nearly every hike allows for at least one bar of service from the summit, but not all hikes are in locations where cell service is available from the parking area. This can be critical for trail mapping and driving directions, so keep this in mind.

Not every park or trail offers visitor-friendly amenities, like restrooms and picnic tables. Some hikes in this book have no amenities at all, but we listed the **amenities** we noticed while hiking the trails and visiting the parks to give you an idea of what to expect, or at the very least give you an indication that you'll need to find a restroom before you reach the trailhead.

The Climb section leads with an overview of the park or nature preserve where the trail is located, including any must-see geological or historical features you won't want to miss. As the section continues, you will learn more about what you will see and at what mileage point, including turns on the trail, connections with other trails, and changes in terrain, as well as benches, picnic tables, and good spots to stop for a snack or to simply savor the views.

Each hike ends with a section of **Miles and Directions,** which features trail junctions, landmarks, and notable surface changes to help ensure you stay on the trail until the end of the hike. As a companion, you'll see a map clearly indicating the route, parking area, local roads, and must-see spots, like overlooks and hikers' shelters. GPS coordinates lead to the parking lot, so you know exactly where to go to park for your summit hike. No need to waste time circling the parking lot, trying to figure out if you are in the right place and the location of the trailhead.

To maximize use of this guide, we suggest you keep it on your night table so that it's the last thing you see at night and the first thing you see when you wake up. These fantastic summit hikes will always be on your mind, as will the need to flip through to find the perfect hike for your next escape to the glorious mountains of Virginia.

ACKNOWLEDGING INDIGENOUS LANDS

This book is intended to support your exploration. Readers will come away with a deeper knowledge of the area, and the opportunity to connect more closely and experience more fully the wonders these lands offer. We respectfully acknowledge that this book covers the traditional land of Indigenous peoples.

Old Rag Scramble

HOW TO PREPARE FOR A SUMMIT HIKE

We all want to reap the rewards of a hike—beautiful views, fresh air, good conversation, colorful flowers. We want to take great photos and get all the likes for our pics. Oh, to dream. To help you get off on the right foot (literally), and keep from twisting it while on a summit hike, here are ten pieces of advice to help ensure success.

1. **Know your limitations.** Many summit hikes can be long, steep, and challenging. The trail surface can be filled with ankle-twisting small rocks. Look within yourself to decide whether you are physically and mentally capable of a hike before setting out for the trail.

2. **Wear proper footwear.** Never has proper footwear with good ankle support been more important than on a summit hike. It can be very easy to slip on rocks or stumble on tree roots, lose your balance, and bring your hike—and your day— to an end. Leave the open-toe sandals and flip-flops at home. Wear proper hiking shoes or boots on a summit hike.

3. **Get an early start.** Not only do many parking lots fill up quickly at some of the most popular trailheads, like McAfee Knob and Tinker Cliffs, but you also don't want to find yourself chasing the sun as you hike back to the trailhead. Without a headlamp, mind you.

4. **Bring a headlamp.** Speaking of headlamps, bring one. Make sure it's fully charged or that you have extra batteries in your daypack. If you get lost or find yourself out on the trail after dark—or maybe before the sun rises—the flashlight on your iPhone is not going to be enough.

5. **Pack more water than you think you need.** Many of these hikes are longer and have more of an elevation gain than your everyday day hike. Bring plenty of water—at least a half-liter of water per hour of moderate hiking activity. It's also wise to bring electrolyte powder packets, like Nuun, to drop into your water bottle to aid with hydration and rehydration.

6. **Fill your daypack with the essentials.** On short hikes, you may be able to manage without snacks or lots of water, but a summit hike requires that you bring all the essentials. These include a navigation aid (could be your phone with a GPS map), sunscreen, a headlamp, a travel first-aid kit, a lighter, water, snacks, extra layers, a whistle, a pocketknife, and an emergency shelter.

7. **Print out maps.** Print out a trail map and directions from the trailhead to your next stop after your hike. Many summit hikes are located in more remote locations where cell service can be unreliable or completely nonexistent. You may not remember how to navigate back home or to the closest town with service after

Mount Rogers Wild Ponies

a hike of several hours, so it's best to print out directions or take a screenshot on your phone.

8. **Let people know where you are.** Tell someone you trust where you're going and when you plan to return. This is always wise advice, but it's especially critical given the more remote nature of some of the hiking trails in this guidebook. Stay on-trail and go where you say you are going that day, just in case anything goes sideways during the hike.

9. **Get versed on parking.** Some hikes begin at parking areas reachable only by way of bumpy, gravelly service roads. When you see the "End State Maintenance" sign, you know you're in for a bumpy ride (literally). If it's highly recommended that only a four-wheel-drive vehicle be used to reach the trailhead, that will be noted in the hike notes.

10. **Consider sunrises and sunsets.** Many of these hikes are optimal for watching a colorful sunrise or sunset. Be sure to bring a headlamp and watch your footing on the trails in the dark. Check the Trail Finder section to find out where to go for sunset or sunrise from a high peak.

TRAIL FINDER

BEST HIKES FOR SUNRISES

Hike 3: Big House Mountain

Hike 7: Hawksbill Summit

Hike 20: Three Ridges

Hike 23: Chestnut Knob

Hike 30: White Rocks

Hike 34: Flat Top

Hike 35: Harkening Hill

Hike 36: McAfee Knob

Hike 37: Pearis Mountain

Hike 39: Sugar Run Mountain

Hike 40: Tinker Mountain

BEST HIKES FOR SUNSETS

Hike 1: Bear Church Rock

Hike 4: Bluff Mountain

Hike 9: Hightop Mountain

Hike 11: Lewis Peak

Hike 13: Mount Pleasant

Hike 15: The Priest

Hike 16: Robertson Mountain

Hike 18: Stony Man Mountain

Hike 22: Buzzard Rock

Hike 25: Haw Orchard Mountain

Hike 27: Middle Knob

Hike 28: Molly's Knob

Hike 32: Bald Knob

Hike 34: Flat Top

BEST HIKES WITH ROCK SCRAMBLES

Hike 1: Bear Church Rock

Hike 2: Bearfence Mountain

Hike: 10: Humpback Rocks

Hike 12: Mary's Rock

Hike 14: Old Rag

Hike 18: Stony Man Mountain

Hike 21: Buffalo Mountain

Hike 25: Haw Orchard Mountain

Hike 32: Bald Knob

Hike 33: Cove Mountain

Hike 34: Flat Top

BEST HIKES FOR CHILDREN

Hike 2: Bearfence Mountain

Hike 5: Cole Mountain

Hike 7: Hawksbill Summit

Hike 8: High Knob

Hike: 10: Humpback Rocks

Hike 12: Mary's Rock

Hike 18: Stony Man Mountain

Hike 21: Buffalo Mountain

Hike 25: Haw Orchard Mountain

Hike 26: High Rocks

Hike 31: Apple Orchard Mountain

Hike 35: Harkening Hill

BEST DOG-FRIENDLY HIKES

Hike 5: Cole Mountain

Hike 19: Terrapin Mountain

Hike 20: Three Ridges

Hike 23: Chestnut Knob

Hike 24: Dickey Knob

Hike 31: Apple Orchard Mountain

Hike 35: Harkening Hill

BEST HIKES FOR SOLITUDE

Hike 1: Bear Church Rock

Hike 16: Robertson Mountain

Hike 17: Spy Rock

Hike 23: Chestnut Knob

Hike 24: Dickey Knob

Hike 29: Mount Rogers

Hike 35: Harkening Hill

Hike 39: Sugar Run Mountain

BEST HIKES FOR WATER FEATURES

Hike 1: Bear Church Rock

Hike 6: Elliott Knob

Hike 14: Old Rag

Hike 16: Robertson Mountain

Hike 19: Terrapin Mountain

Hike 20: Three Ridges

Hike 24: Dickey Knob

BEST HIKES FOR 360-DEGREE VIEWS

Hike 2: Bearfence Mountain

Hike 5: Cole Mountain

Hike 6: Elliott Knob

Hike 8: High Knob

Hike: 10: Humpback Rocks

Hike 12: Mary's Rock

Hike 14: Old Rag

Hike 17: Spy Rock

Hike 21: Buffalo Mountain

Hike 33: Cove Mountain

Hike 38: Sharp Top

BEST HIKES FOR SHELTERS AND CABINS

Hike 1: Bear Church Rock

Hike 3: Big House Mountain

Hike 4: Bluff Mountain

Hike 5: Cole Mountain

Hike 14: Old Rag

Hike 20: Three Ridges

Hike 23: Chestnut Knob

Hike 31: Apple Orchard Mountain

Hike 36: McAfee Knob

Hike 37: Pearis Mountain

Hike 39: Sugar Run Mountain

MAP LEGEND

—81—	Interstate Highway	■	Building/Point of Interest
—285—	US Highway	▲	Campground
—67—	State Highway	○	City/Town
————	County/Forest/Local Road	▬	Lodging
= = = = =	Unpaved Road	▲	Mountain/Peak
+—+—+—+	Railroad	Ⓟ	Parking
■■■■■■	Featured Trail	⤲	Pass
- - - - -	Trail	⊞	Picnic Area
- - · - · - -	State Border	🛈	Ranger Station
～～	Small River/Creek	🎞	Scenic View/Viewpoint
～ ～	Intermittent Stream	⌶	Tower
⬭	Body of Water	①	Trailhead
≋	Waterfall	❷	Visitor Center
⟲	Spring		

SHENANDOAH VALLEY

One of the most peak-dense regions of Virginia is the Shenandoah Valley, thanks largely to 196,000-acre Shenandoah National Park. Many of the peaks are reachable on foot, too. More than 500 miles of hiking trails crisscross the national park, allowing access to the tops of Mary's Rock, Hawksbill Mountain, Bear Church Rock, and many more mountains. Nine of the summit hikes in this guidebook are located within Shenandoah National Park. Some hikes, including Old Rag and Bearfence Mountain, command 360-degree panoramas across the Shenandoah Valley.

While Shenandoah National Park has its share of high peaks, there's more to see in the postcard-perfect Shenandoah Valley, like rock scrambles, wide-open meadows, hikers' shelters, free-flowing rivers, and miles of the white-blazed Appalachian Trail. Hikes to the top of High Knob and Elliott Knob reward with historic—and climbable—fire lookout towers. Both are just three stories tall, but the views from the wraparound catwalks are breathtakingly beautiful.

There's much to behold as you hike to peaks across the 200-mile-long Shenandoah Valley, which includes the Blue Ridge Mountains and Allegheny Mountains. Some summits are near enough to each other that you can check off more than one in a day, like Cole Mountain and Mount Pleasant. It's less than 0.25 mile between the two trailheads. Meanwhile, the Big House Mountain hike includes Little House Mountain, so that's two peaks that you can bag on one big hiking adventure. Lastly, Terrapin Mountain wows with several overlooks, primitive campsites, and a swimming hole that's a refreshing break on a warm summer day.

Every hike in this section has been hand-selected for this guidebook. All hikes inspire with diverse terrain, exhilarating climbs, and far-reaching summit views. Gear up, let's go.

◄ The hike begins on the yellow-blazed Graves Mill Trail with a walk alongside the free-flowing Rapidan River.

1 BEAR CHURCH ROCK

This summit hike at Shenandoah National Park keeps hikers engaged with big mountain views, cascading waterfalls, water crossings, and a primitive cabin.

Start: Parking area at end of Graves Road
Elevation gain: 2,539 feet
Distance: 9.1 miles out and back
Difficulty: Strenuous
Hiking time: 5 to 6 hours
Best season: Year-round
Fees and permits: Free (trailhead is outside the national park; there is no ranger station or fee repository)
Trail contact: Shenandoah National Park, 3655 Hwy. 211 E, Luray; (540) 999-3500; www.nps.gov/shen/
Dogs: Yes
Trail surface: Mostly dirt and rock trails, some wooden steps
Land status: National park
Nearest town: Culpeper
Maps: National Geographic Trails Illustrated Topographic Map 228 (Shenandoah National Park); Map 10: AT in Shenandoah National Park (Central District), PATC, Inc.
Amenities: None
Maximum grade: 28%
Cell service: Reliable
Other trail users: Horses (Graves Mill Trail only)

FINDING THE TRAILHEAD

The trailhead is located at the end of Graves Road, which dead-ends at a circular parking area. When you see the "End State Maintenance" sign, you'll know you are in the right place. Look for the concrete marker for the Graves Mill Trail. **GPS:** N38°26'13.8" / W78°22'01.8"

THE CLIMB

The hike to Bear Church Rock (elevation 3,035 feet) at Shenandoah National Park is one of those hikes that checks several boxes. It's got big mountain views, cascading falls, a log cabin, water crossings, and a swimming hole. There's so much to keep day hikers engaged and dialed in from start to finish. It would be easy to spend a full day in this section of the park.

As you take your first steps from the Graves Mill trailhead, note that the blazes are yellow. At Shenandoah National Park, this means that horses are allowed on the trail. In the same vein, it also means you'll find a wider, less rocky trail—essentially one that is more to the liking of horses and horse hooves.

Nearly from the start, you're walking alongside the cascading Rapidan River. Take in the views and the refreshing burbles of the river. At the 0.5-mile mark, turn left onto the blue-blazed Staunton River Trail. The trail narrows and gets more rocky (of course), but thankfully you'll still enjoy the calming river sounds, as you are now walking alongside the free-flowing Staunton River. As you slowly ascend the trail, notice short spur trails here and there that allow you to walk out to the water, even dip your toes in or splash around to cool off during the hike. Keep your eyes open for a small, gushing waterfall and a watering hole steps off the trail at the 1.1-mile mark. You'll also need to hopscotch

◀ From the Staunton River Trail, it's a cinch to walk out and revel in the tumbling cascades of the Staunton River.

Jones Mountain Cabin, a chestnut log cabin owned and managed by the Potomac Appalachian Trail Club.

across a few streams here and there, including Wilson Run, but well-placed exposed rocks guide your path across at each water crossing.

At the 2.7-mile mark, your time with melodious flowing rivers comes to an end as you bear left onto the blue-blazed Jones Mountain Trail. There is a concrete trail marker, then a dozen wooden steps built into the trail to help manage the climb. At the 3.1-mile mark, turn left again to stay on the Jones Mountain Trail. You'll reach a fork in the trail with a decision to make at the 3.4-mile mark. You can either bear right to continue on to Bear Church Rock, or you can veer left to proceed to Jones Mountain Cabin. A good bet is to stay right to finish the climb and reap the rewards of the scenic overlook, so let's continue. It's a cinch to stop (or not stop) at the cabin on the way back down. But first, get ready to climb more wooden steps built into the hiking trail.

At the 3.9-mile mark, you'll reach another fork in the trail. There is no signage, but thankfully you can see peeks of a mountain overlook 20 or 25 steps farther up the trail on the right. Walk in that direction, and whoa, you're standing on a rocky outcrop taking in huge vistas. Sit and soak them all in. You've earned this moment in time.

Once you've finished, retrace your steps to the fork, then stay right to continue west on the Jones Mountain Trail to Bear Church Rock (the actual summit, not just the overlook). It's only about 0.2 mile, and there are no more views, but you will find several massive boulders that are begging for a climb or a scramble if you are open to the challenge. However, do note that the trail is steep and not especially well-maintained (read: lots of leaves on the trail).

Retrace your steps to the fork again, then stay right to descend the Jones Mountain Trail. At the 4.7-mile mark, turn right to walk 0.3 mile to Jones Mountain Cabin. This chestnut log cabin is owned and managed by the Potomac Appalachian Trail Club (PATC). The cabin sleeps up to ten people on bunks and in a loft space. It can be rented out for a nightly fee, but keep in mind that it is a primitive cabin—there is no electricity, running water, heat, or air-conditioning. Certainly no Wi-Fi. From here, retrace your

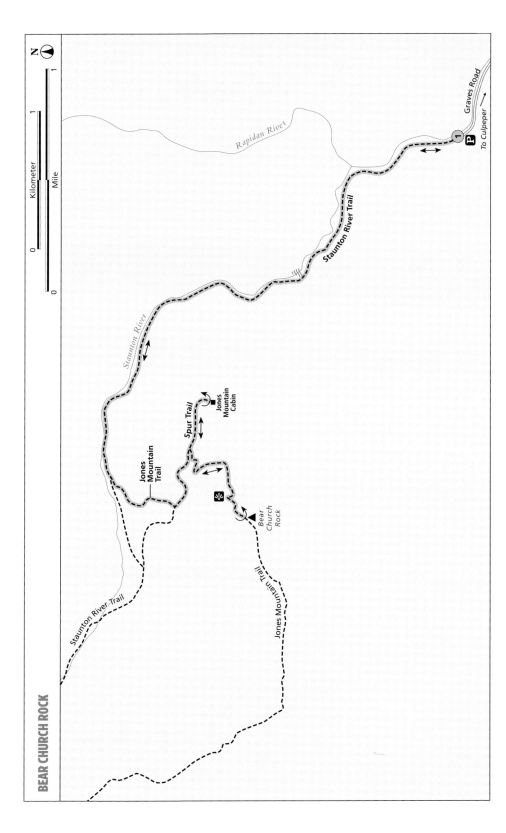

BEAR CHURCH ROCK

Rapidan River

Staunton River

Staunton River Trail

Staunton River Trail

Jones Mountain Trail

Jones Mountain Trail

Spur Trail

Jones Mountain Cabin

Bear Church Rock

Graves Road

To Culpeper

N

Kilometer

Mile

0   1

0   1

Soak in all the mountain views from the rocky outcrop on Bear Church Rock.

steps to the fork, then all the way back to the parking area. Your hike is complete at the 9.1-mile mark.

MILES AND DIRECTIONS

0.0 Begin at the concrete marker for the yellow-blazed Graves Mill Trail.

0.5 Turn left onto the blue-blazed Staunton River Trail.

2.7 Turn left onto the blue-blazed Jones Mountain Trail.

3.1 Turn left to stay on the Jones Mountain Trail.

3.4 Reach a fork in the trail. Stay right for the Jones Mountain Trail.

3.9 Arrive at a fork in the trail. Stay right to reach the overlook in a few more steps. Retrace your steps to the fork, then stay to the right to hike to the actual summit.

4.1 Reach the massive boulders at the summit of Bear Church Rock. Retrace your steps to the fork.

4.3 Turn right to descend the Jones Mountain Trail.

4.7 Turn right onto the spur trail to Jones Mountain Cabin. Retrace your steps.

5.3 Stay right for the Jones Mountain Trail, then retrace your steps to the parking area.

9.1 Arrive back at the parking area. Your hike is complete.

2 BEARFENCE MOUNTAIN

This very short rock scramble leads to spectacular 360-degree panoramas across undulating mountains in the Central District of Shenandoah National Park.

Start: Parking area on Skyline Drive
Elevation gain: 242 feet
Distance: 1.0-mile lollipop
Difficulty: Moderate
Hiking time: About 1 hour
Best season: Year-round
Fees and permits: $$$$
Trail contact: Shenandoah National Park, 3655 Hwy. 211 E., Luray; (540) 999-3500; www.nps.gov/shen/
Dogs: No
Trail surface: Mostly dirt and rock trails, some steps and a rock scramble

Land status: National park
Nearest town: Stanardsville
Maps: National Geographic Trails Illustrated Topographic Map 228 (Shenandoah National Park); Map 10: AT in Shenandoah National Park (Central District), PATC, Inc.
Special considerations: This hike is not considered safe in wet, snowy or icy conditions.
Amenities: None
Maximum grade: 14%
Cell service: Spotty

FINDING THE TRAILHEAD

The hike begins on the opposite side of Skyline Drive from the small parking area at milepost 56.4. **GPS:** N38°27'08.7" / W78°28'01.3"

THE CLIMB

There's a lot to love about a short hike that leads to big views. This is what you get when you choose to hike to the summit of Bearfence Mountain (elevation 3,553 feet) in the popular Central District of Shenandoah National Park. On a clear day, the rolling mountains go on and on. The 360-degree views are absolutely sensational. You'll be glad you decided on this summit hike.

This hike is only 1.0 mile, on a loop that includes the Bearfence Mountain Trail and the Appalachian Trail, but this short distance can be deceptive. This is not an easy hike, especially as you near the top and arrive at a rock scramble. Many hikers have reached this point only to turn around, certain they cannot continue on to the rocky summit, not even for such big views.

The trail begins with a few dozen steps built into the Bearfence Mountain Trail. You will quickly arrive at a four-way intersection with the white-blazed Appalachian Trail at the 0.1-mile mark. Continue straight ahead and climb more steps on your way to the sizable rocky outcrop.

Just before the 0.3-mile mark, you will reach several massive boulders that block your way to the top. Yes, you have already reached the rock scramble. The boulders are marked with blue blazes, but you may think that this can't be the trail. It is. Take a breath and get ready to use your hands, feet, knees, and elbows to navigate large, jagged rocks. You may need to hoist yourself up onto the rocks.

You will start to see traces of sensational views. It's so close. Dig deep; you can tackle this one. The rock scramble is just over 0.1 mile. Once you reach the top, settle in to

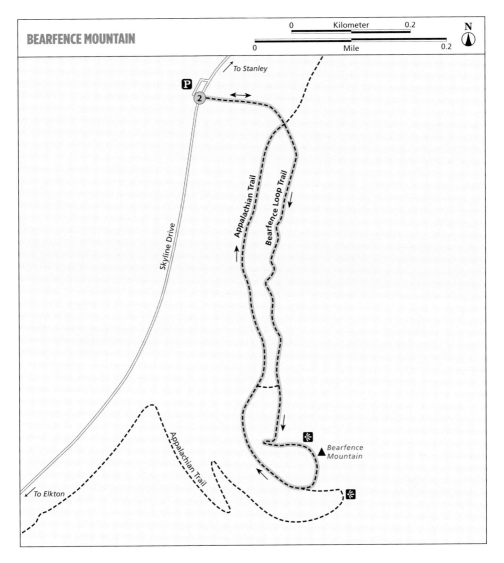

0   Kilometer   0.2

N

0   Mile   0.2

To Stanley

P

Appalachian Trail

Bearfence Loop Trail

Skyline Drive

Appalachian Trail

Bearfence Mountain

To Elkton

rehydrate and revel in the far-reaching vistas. It will not be easy to leave the vista-laden summit of Bearfence Mountain and return to your car.

The rock scramble ends near the 0.5-mile mark. A few steps later, make a right turn onto a short connector trail. In a few more steps, turn right again, this time onto the Appalachian Trail. From here, it's a shady downhill trail of dirt, rocks, and gravel. At the 0.9-mile mark you'll return to the four-way junction from earlier in the hike. Turn left to return to the parking lot.

◀ Kids and adults alike will enjoy scrambling up, over, and around big and small rocks to reach the top of this mountain summit.

Plan to use hands, feet, arms, elbows, and knees to skillfully navigate the rock scramble to reach the top of Bearfence Mountain.

MILES AND DIRECTIONS

0.0 Begin across Skyline Drive from the parking area at milepost 56.4.

0.1 Reach a four-way intersection. Continue straight ahead on the blue-blazed Bearfence Mountain Trail.

0.3 Arrive at a rock scramble to the summit.

0.4 Reach the summit of Bearfence Mountain.

0.5 Turn right onto a blue-blazed spur trail, then turn right onto the Appalachian Trail.

0.9 Turn left at the four-way intersection.

1.0 Cross Skyline Drive. Arrive back at the parking area. Your hike is complete.

OPTION

For an easier hike, though not necessarily a shorter hike, opt for the Bearfence Viewpoint Hike, which wows with 180-degree views. This out-and-back hike begins at the same trailhead but bypasses the rock scramble and clocks in at just under 1.0 mile.

For this hike, turn right at the 0.1-mile mark onto the Appalachian Trail at the four-way junction. From here, it's a slow climb until you turn left at the 0.4-mile mark onto the connector trail. You'll quickly see a trail marker. Turn right in a few more steps to reach the viewpoint. Once you've taken in all the views, retrace your steps to the parking area.

You will realize all your efforts to reach the top were worth it when you get your first look at the spectacular vistas from atop Bearfence Mountain.

3 BIG HOUSE MOUNTAIN

This hike can be ruthless at times, but you are richly rewarded with views from the tops of both Big House Mountain and Little House Mountain. This hike is one to add to your bucket list.

Start: House Mountain Reserve parking area
Elevation gain: 3,219 feet
Distance: 10.7 miles out and back
Difficulty: Strenuous
Hiking time: 6.5 to 8 hours
Best season: Year-round
Fees and permits: Free
Trail contact: George Washington and Jefferson National Forest (Glenwood-Pedlar Ranger District), 27 Ranger Ln., Natural Bridge

Station; (540) 291-2188; www.fs.usda.gov/detail/gwj
Dogs: Yes
Trail surface: Mostly grass, dirt, and rock trails, some rock scrambles
Land status: Nature reserve
Nearest town: Lexington
Maps: National Geographic Trails Illustrated Topographic Map 789 (Lexington, Blue Ridge Mountains)
Amenities: Privy at the saddle
Maximum grade: 28%
Cell service: Reliable

FINDING THE TRAILHEAD

The hike begins from the front of the designated parking area for House Mountain Reserve on Saddle Ridge Road (which is the only place to park for this hike). There is a trail kiosk and a large trail map. **GPS:** N37°48'40.8" / W79°31'50.3"

THE CLIMB

To set expectations: This may be one of the most challenging hikes you will ever do in Virginia, but it may also be among the most rewarding thanks to two mountain summits. This 10.7-mile hike includes overlooks from Big House Mountain (elevation 3,645 feet) and Little House Mountain (elevation 3,386 feet). There's even a bonus overlook near a geological oddity called Table Rock. Bring lots of water and snacks. Maybe even bring celebratory champagne. You will need them all. This hike includes steps on four separate trails within 986-acre House Mountain Reserve, which was once owned by White's Truck Stop (now White's Travel Center). In 1989 the Virginia Outdoors Foundation swooped in to purchase the land when it was put up for sale in order to ensure the acreage was retained and available for public recreational use.

Turn left as you exit the parking lot; the ascent begins now. From here, it's 0.1 mile to Trail Head Lane, as it's marked on the trail map. Essentially, this is still Saddle Ridge Road. You'll start to see signs noting public access for House Mountain Reserve, but also that motor vehicles are not permitted (except for residents). You are now walking along a gravel road that provides access to a half-dozen homes. At the 0.7-mile mark, you'll reach the last two private homes and a metal gate across the road. Walk around the gate and the trail becomes House Mountain Trail, though there are no blazes. From here, it's a gradual forested ascent to the saddle at the 2.4-mile mark.

The saddle was once a fruit orchard and is now the starting point for the red-blazed Big House Mountain Trail and the blue-blazed Little House Mountain Trail. The area

Top: A few fun and easy rock scrambles welcome hikers on the approach to the overlook for Little House Mountain.

Bottom: A wooden hikers' shelter sits at the saddle between Big House Mountain and Little House Mountain.

Get ready to revel in northeast-facing views from the rocky outcrop at the end of the Big House Mountain Trail.

Soak up big mountain views from a rocky outcrop southwest of Table Rock. Some call this Goat Point Overlook.

can get overgrown with tall grasses, so it's best to wear long pants on this hike. Continue west and you will reach a wooden hikers' shelter with a fire pit and a privy at the 2.5-mile mark. It's a nice spot to catch your breath before the climb up Big House Mountain.

Follow the red diamonds up Big House Mountain. This section is *very* steep, but it's not particularly lengthy. At the 3.1-mile mark, you will reach a sign for Table Rock. Stay left and follow the orange diamonds. Rock scrambles to the top require full access to hands, arms, knees, and feet. Thankfully, it's less than 0.1 mile to the top, where you'll reach a wooden trail sign. Turn left here for the short walk to the overlook, which you'll reach at the 3.3-mile mark. Some call this overlook Goat Point Overlook—named for a local goat that at one time hung out here for hiker handouts—and the west-facing vistas are simply spectacular. Retrace your steps to the sign, then follow the orange diamonds to Table Rock, a curious rock formation set atop a boulder. It does in fact look like a lopsided table.

At the 3.6-mile mark, the trail dead-ends at the Big House Mountain Trail. Turn left to proceed to the overlook, but not before passing a small abandoned building of unknown origin or purpose. You will then see a sign that reads "Overlook," which would appear to indicate that an overlook is imminent, but it is not. Continue following the red blazes north for another 0.4 mile. It's a gentle ascent and the trail will end at a rocky overlook with big east-facing mountain views. Retrace your steps to the Big House Mountain Trail sign, which you will reach at the 4.4-mile mark. Instead of turning right, which would take you back to Table Rock, continue straight ahead to follow the red blazes. At the 4.7-mile mark, turn left for a steep descent back to the saddle.

You will arrive at the saddle at the 5.3-mile mark. From here, follow the blue-blazed Little House Mountain Trail. This forested section starts out mellow, but soon becomes arduous. Thankfully, a wide-open view turns up at the 5.6-mile mark, then a rocky outcrop appears at the 5.8-mile mark. The latter, in particular, is an ideal spot to take a break and rehydrate. Much of this trail is quite narrow, but it does flatten out near the top and even engages hikers with a fun rock scramble. You'll arrive at the overlook at the 6.8-mile mark. At this point, after hiking to two summits, you may not be especially eager for the rocky return hike to the parking lot, so sit and savor the views of the mountains and working farms in the valley below. Once you've rehydrated, refueled, and soaked it all in, retrace your steps to the saddle, then back down to the parking area. Your hike is complete at the 10.7-mile mark.

MILES AND DIRECTIONS

0.0 Begins from the dedicated parking lot on Saddle Ridge Road.

0.1 Continue straight ahead onto Trail Head Lane. Follow the green signs for House Mountain Reserve.

0.7 Reach an iron gate restricting motor vehicles. Walk around the iron gate to continue on the trail, which becomes House Mountain Trail.

2.4 Arrive at the saddle between Big House Mountain and Little House Mountain. Continue west for the red-blazed Big House Mountain Trail.

2.5 Reach a hikers' shelter with a fire pit and privy.

3.1 Bear left and follow the orange diamonds to Table Rock Overlook.

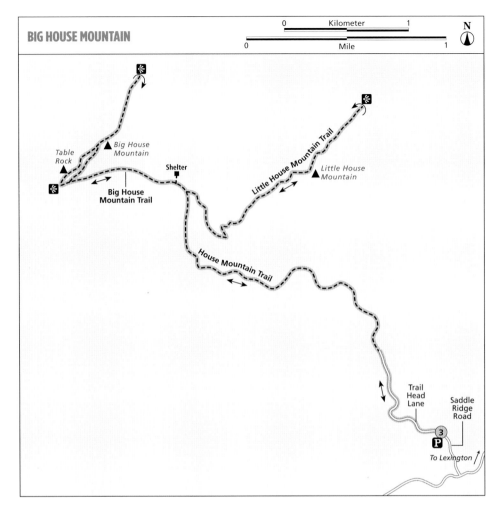

3.3 Reach Table Rock Overlook. Retrace your steps to the trail sign, then proceed to Table Rock.

3.4 Arrive at Table Rock.

3.6 Turn left onto the Big House Mountain Trail.

4.0 Arrive at the rocky outcrop for views from Big House Mountain. Retrace your steps to the trail sign.

4.4 Continue straight ahead on the Big House Mountain Trail.

4.7 Turn left to return to the saddle.

5.3 Connect with the blue-blazed Little House Mountain Trail.

5.8 Arrive at a rocky outcrop for south-facing views.

6.8 Reach the rocky overlook for views from Little House Mountain. Retrace your steps to the saddle, then on to the parking area.

10.7 Arrive back at the parking area. Your hike is complete.

4 BLUFF MOUNTAIN

The hike to the top of Bluff Mountain includes a hikers' shelter, as well as a couple of surprises, including remains of a former fire tower and a historical marker of tribute to a child who went missing while collecting firewood more than one hundred years ago.

Start: Punch Bowl Mountain Overlook
Elevation gain: 1,414 feet
Distance: 4.3 miles out and back
Difficulty: Moderate
Hiking time: 3 to 4 hours
Best season: Year-round
Fees and permits: Free
Trail contact: George Washington and Jefferson National Forest (Glenwood-Pedlar Ranger District), 27 Ranger Ln., Natural Bridge Station; (540) 291-2188; www.fs.usda .gov/detail/gwj

Dogs: Yes
Trail surface: Mostly dirt and gravel trails
Land status: National forest
Nearest town: Buena Vista
Maps: National Geographic Trails Illustrated Topographic Map 789 (Lexington, Blue Ridge Mountains)
Amenities: Privy at hikers' shelter
Maximum grade: 22%
Cell service: Spotty (no service at the trailhead)

FINDING THE TRAILHEAD

The trailhead is located across the Blue Ridge Parkway from the Punch Bowl Mountain Overlook at milepost 51.7. You'll find more of a pullout than a parking lot here, since there are no actual lined spaces, though a half-dozen cars can safely park. **GPS:** N37°40'26.9" / W79°20'03.5"

THE CLIMB

The trail to the top of Bluff Mountain is an easy one to find, one of several hikes with a starting point along the iconic Blue Ridge Parkway. Before you begin, take in the east-facing views across the George Washington National Forest, though do note that they are largely obscured by very tall trees.

Walk across the Blue Ridge Parkway to the trailhead, which is just north of the parking area. From here, climb a southbound stretch of the white-blazed Appalachian Trail. The hike is straightforward, steadily ascending 2.0 miles until you reach the top of Bluff Mountain (elevation 3,330 feet).

Within the first few steps you'll see a trail sign indicating that the Punch Bowl Shelter is just 0.4 mile up the trail (emphasis on *up* the trail). While this is a climb all the way to the top, it's not ruthless, but manageable and rather scenic, especially with spring wildflowers in bloom. If you want to check out the hikers' shelter, turn right onto a spur trail at the 0.4-mile mark. It's 0.2 mile to the Punch Bowl Shelter. The shelter is a typical lean-to shelter that's common on the Appalachian Trail. The basic setup includes a picnic table, a privy, and a fire pit, as well as plenty of space for tents.

From the shelter, retrace your steps, then continue following the white blazes up the Appalachian Trail. You'll literally climb at the 1.1-mile mark when you reach a dozen wooden steps built into the hiking trail. As you proceed, get ready for a half-dozen

Midway to the top of Bluff Mountain you'll find a dozen or so wooden steps built into the forested hiking trail.

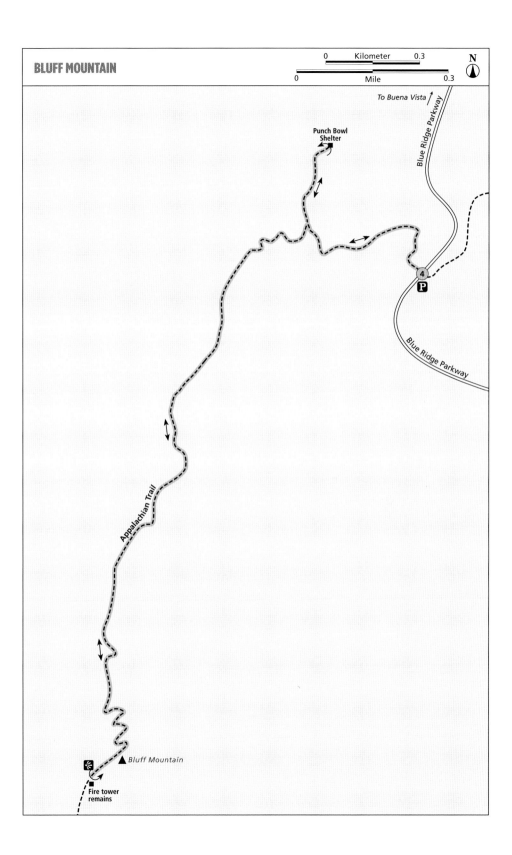

BLUFF MOUNTAIN

0   Kilometer   0.3

0   Mile   0.3

N

To Buena Vista

Blue Ridge Parkway

Punch Bowl
Shelter

4
P

Blue Ridge Parkway

Appalachian Trail

Bluff Mountain

Fire tower
remains

Top: Just 0.4 mile into the hike is a spur trail that leads to the Punch Bowl Shelter, a typical lean-to hikers' shelter that is common along the Appalachian Trail.

Bottom: Soak in the far-reaching views across the Blue Ridge Mountains from the top of Bluff Mountain.

The hike to the top of Bluff Mountain begins across the Blue Ridge Parkway from the parking area for the Punch Bowl Mountain Overlook at milepost 51.7.

switchbacks at the 2.0-mile mark. You're getting close now. Then, at the 2.3-mile mark, you'll arrive at the summit and its magnificent far-reaching views.

Interestingly, you've stumbled upon what was once a fire tower used by the US Forest Service. All that's left is some of the foundation and a few steps. Today the concrete foundation and steps serve as little more than places to sit, snack, and ogle the spectacular west-facing vistas across the Blue Ridge Mountains.

At the summit, keep your eyes peeled for a historical marker of tribute to Ottie Cline Powell. As the story goes, four-year-old Powell was found dead here in 1892, nearly five months after wandering away from Tower Hill Schoolhouse to collect firewood. From the top of Bluff Mountain, retrace your steps to the trailhead. Your hike is complete at the 4.3-mile mark.

MILES AND DIRECTIONS

0.0 Begin across the Blue Ridge Parkway from the Punch Bowl Mountain Overlook.

0.4 Turn right onto a spur trail for the Punch Bowl Shelter.

0.6 Arrive at the Punch Bowl Shelter. Retrace your steps to the Appalachian Trail.

0.8 Reconnect with the Appalachian Trail and continue southbound.

2.3 Reach the summit of Bluff Mountain. Retrace your steps to the trailhead.

4.3 Arrive back at the trailhead. Your hike is complete.

You'll reach the top of Cole Mountain within the first mile of this scenic hike.

5 COLE MOUNTAIN

You'll feel like Julie Andrews from *The Sound of Music* when you reach the large, grassy, meadow-like summit of Cole Mountain.

Start: First parking area on Wiggins Spring Road
Elevation gain: 1,319 feet
Distance: 6.3-mile loop
Difficulty: Moderate
Hiking time: 3 to 4 hours
Best season: Mar–Nov (due to passability of Wiggins Spring Road)
Fees and permits: Free
Trail contact: George Washington and Jefferson National Forest (Glenwood-Pedlar Ranger District), 27 Ranger Ln., Natural Bridge Station; (540) 291-2188; www.fs.usda.gov/detail/gwj
Dogs: Yes

Trail surface: Mostly dirt and gravel trails
Land status: National forest
Nearest town: Buena Vista
Maps: National Geographic Trails Illustrated Topographic Map 789 (Lexington, Blue Ridge Mountains)
Amenities: Privy at hikers' shelter
Maximum grade: 20%
Cell service: Spotty
Special considerations: The gravel road leading to the parking area is bumpy and not well-suited for sedans. A four-wheel-drive vehicle is recommended.

FINDING THE TRAILHEAD

The trailhead is located across from the first parking lot you reach, on the left, about 4.5 miles down Wiggins Spring Road. **GPS:** N37°45′34.4″ / W79°11′42.6″

THE CLIMB

There's a lot to love about the climb to the grassy summit of Cole Mountain, but it's certainly not the drive to the parking lot. The drive along gravelly, bumpy Wiggins Spring Road may be the biggest challenge of your day, despite the overall 1,319-foot elevation gain you'll see over the course of this scenic loop hike to and beyond the top of Cole Mountain (elevation 3,927 feet).

To be honest, if you want to make this hike short and sweet, you can tackle Cole Mountain as a 1.8-mile out-and-back hike with an overall elevation gain of just 400 feet, but if you survived the drive in, you may as well tackle the full 6.3-mile loop. However, the shorter option is nice to have in your back pocket when hiking with smaller children with little legs.

From the parking area, look for a green marker for the Appalachian Trail on the opposite side of the road. There are two hiking trails that start here. Slowly ascend 400 feet into the George Washington National Forest by way of the white-blazed hiking trail on the left. In short order you will reach the highpoint of Cole Mountain (aka Cold Mountain), but there is no rocky summit. It's a wide-open meadow—a bald, really. It's a massive open space with plentiful mountain views. You may begin to feel like Julie Andrews. It's very *Sound of Music*. There are several large rocks that are just right for a lunch or snack break.

Continue following the white blazes across the top of Cole Mountain. At the 1.6-mile mark, the trail exits the openness of the grassy meadow and descends back into the forest.

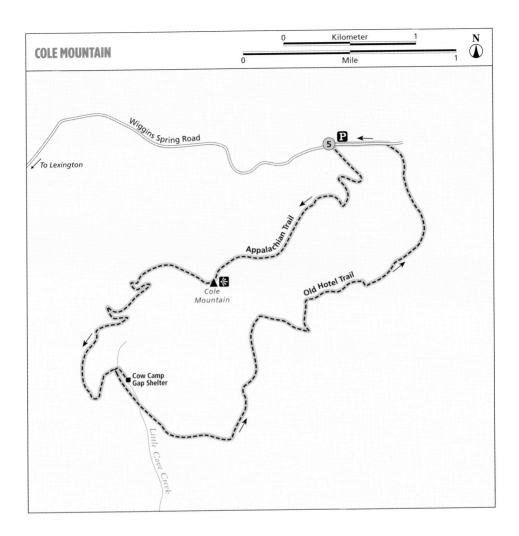

0   Kilometer   1

0   Mile   1

N

Wiggins Spring Road

To Lexington

5 P

Appalachian Trail

Cole Mountain

Old Hotel Trail

Cow Camp Gap Shelter

Little Cow Creek

A rocky outcrop appears at the 2.2-mile mark. Get ready to savor spectacular west-facing views across neighboring mountains. In a few more steps, you'll reach a fork in the trail, as well as a trail sign. Turn left here for the Old Hotel Trail. Follow blue blazes in the direction of Cow Camp Gap Shelter and Hog Camp Gap. At the 3.1-mile mark, cross over a small stream to reach Cow Camp Gap Shelter, a lean-to shelter, which includes a picnic table, a privy, and a fire ring.

Retrace your steps to the Old Hotel Trail and turn left to continue on. You'll keep descending until the 3.6-mile mark, but then it's time to make up all that elevation loss, so get ready to start climbing again. The trail opens back up at the 4.8-mile mark. Here you'll see several fire rings for backpackers and tent camping. You'll reach another fork in

◀ Top: The trailhead is located a few steps from the parking area. Look for the green Appalachian Trail marker.

Bottom: Take time to explore the Cow Camp Gap Shelter for backpackers near the middle of this forested loop hike.

Savor all the far-reaching views from the large meadow-like highpoint of Cole Mountain.

the trail at the 6.0-mile mark. Stay left to proceed on the Old Hotel Trail. As you hike on, you'll start to see hikers ascending Mount Pleasant just a few steps to the right on a parallel trail.

At the 6.1-mile mark, the trail exits onto the gravel Wiggins Spring Road. From this point, it's another 0.2 mile to reach the Cole Mountain parking area and complete the hike.

MILES AND DIRECTIONS

0.0 Begin on the opposite side of Wiggins Spring Road from the parking area. You will see a sign for the Appalachian Trail, as well as two trails. The Appalachian Trail is on the left.

0.9 Arrive at the meadow-like summit of Cole Mountain. Follow the white blazes across the top of the mountain.

1.6 The trail descends into the forest.

2.2	Reach a rocky outcrop for scenic west-facing mountain views. In a few more, steps, turn left for the Old Hotel Trail.
3.1	Cross over a small stream to explore Cow Camp Gap Shelter. Retrace your steps to the Old Hotel Trail, then turn left to continue on.
4.8	Arrive at a clearing with fire rings for campsites.
6.0	The trail splits in two; veer left for the Old Hotel Trail.
6.1	Exit onto Wiggins Spring Road. Slowly ascend until you reach the parking area on the right.
6.3	Arrive back at the parking area. Your hike is complete.

OPTION

From the trailhead, ascend the Appalachian Trail to reach the grassy meadow atop Cole Mountain after 0.9 mile. Revel in the views, then retrace your steps to the parking area to complete a short, but photo-worthy 1.8-mile hike.

The one-time fire lookout tower at the top of Elliott Knob is a welcome sight after climbing 4.6 miles to reach the panorama-filled summit.

6 ELLIOTT KNOB

This strenuous hike heaps big rewards on worthy hikers that make the climb to Elliott Knob to see one of the few remaining fire lookouts in Virginia.

Start: Parking area on Little Calf Pasture Highway
Elevation gain: 2,434 feet
Distance: 9.2 miles out and back
Difficulty: Strenuous
Hiking time: 5 to 6 hours
Best season: Year-round
Fees and permits: Free
Trail contact: George Washington and Jefferson National Forest (Glenwood-Pedlar Ranger District), 27 Ranger Ln., Natural Bridge

Station; (540) 291-2188; www.fs.usda.gov/detail/gwj
Dogs: Yes
Trail surface: Mostly dirt, grass, rock, and gravel trails
Land status: National forest
Nearest town: Staunton
Maps: National Geographic Trails Illustrated Topographic Map 791 (Staunton, Shenandoah Mountain)
Amenities: None
Maximum grade: 24%
Cell service: Fairly reliable

FINDING THE TRAILHEAD

The trailhead is located at a small parking area on Little Calf Pasture Highway, 0.2 mile south of the entrance to the Shenandale Gun Club. There's room for only two or three cars, so the lot can be easy to miss (keep your eyes open for an iron gate across a fire road); if this lot is full, you'll need to find another hike for the day. **GPS:** N38°09'40.7" / W79°16'10.8"

THE CLIMB

At an elevation of 4,463 feet, Elliott Knob is the highest point in Augusta County. It's also the tallest peak in Virginia's Shenandoah Valley. This hike rewards with spectacular 360-degree views across the George Washington National Forest from atop the three-story one-time fire tower that sits on Elliott Knob, but you'll need to dig deep to be worthy of the spoils, particularly in the last 1.5 miles in full sun as you hike to the top. Thankfully, there are a few diversions on the way up, including a cascading creek, a small pond, and several primitive campsites.

From the small parking area on Little Calf Pasture Highway, proceed past the iron gate, which restricts vehicles from motoring along what is now exclusively a hiking trail, the Falls Hollow Trail. You will see a wooden trail sign on the right side of the trail within the first few steps of the hike. From here, it's a gentle ascent along a mostly grass and gravel trail, but don't let this hike fool you. This is merely a warm-up for what's to come later on in the hike. At the 1.5-mile mark, keep your eyes open for a short spur trail that leads to the refreshing cascades of Falls Hollow Run. Continue on and you will pass a couple of small waterfalls, too. In all, you'll walk alongside Falls Hollow Run for 0.5 mile. Savor every moment. The climb is coming.

At the 2.2-mile mark, you'll reach a switchback. The trail narrows and jogs to the left. Follow the yellow diamonds (the first trail markers of any kind that you will see) as you continue ascending along the Falls Hollow Trail. The trail ends at the 3.0-mile mark at

At the 2.2-mile mark, look for a switchback as the trail narrows and yellow diamonds lead the way for the next 0.8 mile.

a trail sign indicating a right turn to proceed to Elliott Knob. You're now in full sun on a gravel service road that appears to ascend to heaven; it is very steep in some sections and seems to just keep going and going. This last 1.5-mile section is the definition of unrelenting. Take lots of water breaks. You will need them.

The gravel road actually leads to transmission towers for a local television and radio station. It's impossible to imagine how even a four-wheel-drive vehicle makes the climb up this road. At the 4.1-mile mark, the gravel road flattens as you arrive at a small pond. Take a break, but you've still got 0.5 mile to go to reach the historic fire tower.

ELLIOTT KNOB

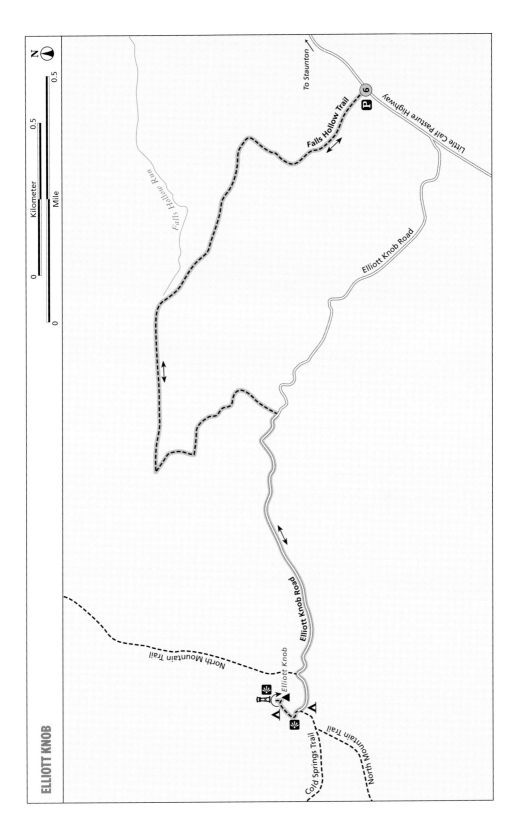

N

Kilometer
0   0.5

Mile
0   0.5

To Staunton

Falls Hollow Trail

P 6

Little Calf Pasture Highway

Falls Hollow Run

Elliott Knob Road

North Mountain Trail

Elliott Knob

Elliott Knob Road

Cold Springs Trail

North Mountain Trail

Early in this hike, enjoy the refreshing cascades and small waterfalls on Falls Hollow Run.

At the 4.2-mile mark, you'll pass the North Mountain Trail, which sets off to the right. Just keep moving on up the gravel road. You're getting close. You'll reach a trail marker on the left at the 4.4-mile mark, but this is for the North Mountain and Cold Springs Trails. Take a break and explore several shaded campsites in this forested section. Keep walking and the trail narrows for your final steps to Elliott Knob. But first, pause at the 4.5-mile mark for a small, rocky overlook on the left that wows with west-facing views. At the 4.6-mile mark, you can see the fire tower. At last. As you close in on the tower, you'll see a large grassy area in front of the fire tower with a big stone fire pit. There's plenty of room to set up tents here, too, to enjoy a good night's sleep at the summit and a colorful morning sunrise. What a wonderful reward.

The one-time fire tower is surrounded by a metal chain-link fence, but the gate is open. Hikers can carefully climb the forty-plus metal steps to the wraparound catwalk on the fire tower to revel in far-reaching 360-degree panoramas. You can even step inside the cab of the fire tower, as that glass door is left open, too. A still-standing fire tower in Virginia is rare, so soak up all the views from one of Virginia's highest peaks. On the way down, peek into the wooded area to the left of the fire tower and you'll see a few more shaded campsites with fire rings. From here, retrace your steps to your vehicle and celebrate completion of this strenuous summit hike.

Climb forty-plus steps to walk the wraparound catwalk of the one-time fire tower. Soak up gorgeous mountain views in all directions.

MILES AND DIRECTIONS

0.0 Begin at a small parking area on Little Calf Pasture Highway. Walk around the metal gate and begin hiking on the Falls Hollow Trail.

1.5 A short spur trail leads to Falls Hollow Run. Retrace your steps to the Falls Hollow Trail.

2.2 Turn left at a switchback to continue ascending the Falls Hollow Trail.

3.0 The trail ends at a gravel service road. Turn right to continue to Elliott Knob.

4.1 A small pond sits on the right side of the trail.

4.2 Reach the junction with the North Mountain Trail, but stay left to proceed to Elliott Knob.

4.4 Arrive at a trail marker and primitive campsites on the left. Continue straight ahead.

4.5 Enjoy wide-open views from a small rocky overlook on the left side of the trail.

4.6 Arrive at the fire tower at Elliott Knob. Climb to the top of the tower for panoramas. Also, check out the campsites in front of and to the left of the former lookout tower. From here, retrace your steps to your vehicle.

9.2 Arrive back at the parking area. Your hike is complete.

Take time to admire the colorful asters and goldenrods in the final steps of your hike to Hawksbill Summit.

7 HAWKSBILL SUMMIT

There are three ways to reach Hawksbill Summit, the highest peak at Shenandoah National Park. This hike pairs a mild ascent with scenic panoramas and curious terrain, like rock scrambles and forested trails.

Start: Hawksbill Gap parking area
Elevation gain: 771 feet
Distance: 2.8-mile loop
Difficulty: Moderate
Hiking time: 1.5 to 2 hours
Best season: Year-round
Fees and permits: $$$$
Trail contact: Shenandoah National Park, 3655 Hwy. 211 E., Luray; (540) 999-3500; www.nps.gov/shen/
Dogs: Yes
Trail surface: Mostly dirt and gravel trails, small rock scrambles, some tree roots to navigate

Land status: National park
Nearest town: Sperryville (east) or Luray (west)
Maps: National Geographic Trails Illustrated Topographic Map 228 (Shenandoah National Park); Map 10: AT in Shenandoah National Park (Central District), PATC, Inc.
Amenities: None
Maximum grade: 18%
Cell service: Spotty

FINDING THE TRAILHEAD

Park at the Hawksbill Gap parking area on the west side of Skyline Drive at milepost 45.6. **GPS:** N38°33'22.43034" / W78 °23'13.09970

THE CLIMB

Hawksbill Summit (elevation 4,051 feet) is the highest point at Shenandoah National Park. It's also among the most popular destinations in the park, maybe due to the relative ease of reaching the rewarding vistas across the Shenandoah Valley and Blue Ridge Mountains.

There are three different routes to ascend Hawksbill Summit. To be clear, however, the shortest path is certainly not the easiest route to the top. In fact, the 1.6-mile out-and-back hike on the blue-blazed Lower Hawksbill Trail is a real slog to the stone observation platform. At 2.8 miles, the loop hike, which includes steps on the Appalachian Trail, is longer than the out-and-back hike, but the elevation gain is more manageable with lots of flat stretches, especially when navigated counterclockwise.

From the Hawksbill Gap parking area, follow the trail on the right for the loop hike (the left-most trail is for the out-and-back hike on the Lower Hawksbill Trail). This spur trail quickly bisects the white-blazed Appalachian Trail. Turn left at the concrete trail marker to pick up the southbound route.

From here, there is a mild ascent, then a flat section, then a mild ascent (repeat, repeat). In summer the trail is verdant with plenty of low-growth plants and ferns decorating the shady, dirt path through the woods. Just before the 0.5-mile mark, you'll reach a talus slope, an enormous sloping pile of rocks that slides across the trail from the left-hand side, covering the trail as it continues down Hawksbill Mountain.

Pack a lunch for your hike to Hawksbill Summit. On the way to the top you'll pass Byrds Nest Shelter #2, a day-use shelter with a picnic table.

In a few more steps, you'll see a second rocky slope, then a third. The fourth one will require an easy scramble. Watch your footing as some rocks can be loose. As you reenter the shady forest, you will reach a fork in the trail just after the 1.0 mile mark. Keep left for the blue-blazed Salamander Trail, a segment of trail named for the Shenandoah salamander, an endangered species found only in Shenandoah National Park.

At the 1.9-mile mark, turn left onto the gravel Hawksbill Fire Road. Turn left again at the concrete trail marker onto Lower Hawksbill Trail. Byrds Nest Shelter #2 soon comes into view. This day-use shelter houses one picnic table. In summer, cheery asters and goldenrods welcome hikers in the final ascent to the summit. A flat, northwest-facing viewpoint is on the left. To your right, a large rock outcropping beckons hikers

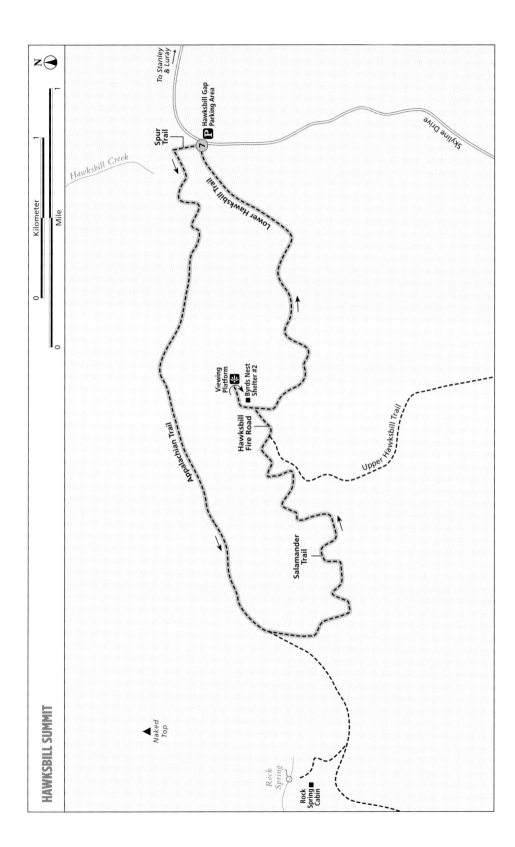

HAWKSBILL SUMMIT

N

Kilometer
Mile

To Stanley & Luray

Skyline Drive

Hawksbill Gap Parking Area

Spur Trail

Hawksbill Creek

Lower Hawksbill Trail

Appalachian Trail

Upper Hawksbill Trail

Viewing Platform

Byrds Nest Shelter #2

Hawksbill Fire Road

Salamander Trail

Naked Top

Rock Spring

Rock Spring Cabin

to scramble to the top for elevated views. A trail sign notes that the summit—as well as an actual viewing platform—is just 50 yards up the trail.

From Hawksbill Summit, take in 270-degree views. To the west is Massanutten Mountain, while Old Rag Mountain proudly stands to the northeast. Take a seat on the rocky out-crop to enjoy the views or investigate the curious sundial at the viewing platform. To return to the parking lot, retrace your steps to the first trail marker, then turn left to hike down the Lower Hawksbill Trail. Watch your footing as it's a relatively steep descent with lots of loose rocks.

At last, Hawksbill Summit is just 50 yards from this point. This is a welcome sign following a relatively steep ascent to reach the highest peak at Shenandoah National Park.

MILES AND DIRECTIONS

0.0 Begin at the Hawksbill Gap parking area on the west side of Skyline Drive and choose the trail that leads off to the right.

0.1 Turn left to connect with the white-blazed Appalachian Trail.

0.5 Cross three or four small fields of mid-size rocks over a span of 300 yards.

1.1 The trail splits. Veer left to continue on the Salamander Trail, which leads to the summit.

1.9 The trail connects with the Hawksbill Fire Road, so turn left. In a few more steps, turn left again onto Lower Hawksbill Trail. The Byrds Nest Shelter #2 comes into view on the right.

2.0 Arrive at Hawksbill Summit, including the Hawksbill Viewing Platform.

2.1 Walking away from the summit, turn left at the first trail marker to descend the steep and rocky Lower Hawksbill Trail to the parking area.

2.8 Arrive back at the Hawksbill Gap parking area. Your hike is complete. Celebrate.

OPTION

You can also reach Hawksbill Summit by way of the Upper Hawksbill Trail, which can be accessed from the Upper Hawksbill parking area at milepost 46.7. This 2.1-mile out-and-back hike guides visitors to the summit from a higher starting elevation point (nearly 300 feet higher).

From the trailhead, walk straight ahead, then turn right at a concrete trail marker near the 0.7-mile mark for the Hawksbill Fire Road. Just past the 0.9-mile mark, you'll see another trail marker. Turn right to join the Salamander Trail. At the 1.0-mile mark, you'll reach one more trail marker. Turn left for the Lower Hawksbill Trail and the final ascent to the summit.

Settle in and revel in the spectacular far-reaching views across the Shenandoah Valley and Blue Ridge Mountains.

HIGH KNOB
FIRE DETECTION TOWER
SHENANDOAH MOUNTAIN ELEVATION 4107
THIS RIDGE IS THE STATE LINE BETWEEN
VIRGINIA AND WEST VIRGINIA
GEORGE WASHINGTON
NATIONAL FOREST

8 HIGH KNOB

This moderate hike near Harrisonburg leads to a restored historic fire tower and sensational 360-degree panoramas across the Blue Ridge Mountains.

Start: Parking area on US 33
Elevation gain: 682 feet
Distance: 2.8 miles out and back
Difficulty: Moderate
Hiking time: 2 to 2.5 hours
Best season: Year-round
Fees and permits: Free
Trail contact: George Washington and Jefferson National Forest (Lee Ranger District), 95 Railroad Ave., Edinburg; (540) 984-4101; www.fs.usda.gov/detail/gwj

Dogs: Yes
Trail surface: Mostly dirt and rock trails
Land status: National forest
Nearest town: Harrisonburg
Maps: National Geographic Trails Illustrated Topographic Map 792 (Massanutten, Great North Mountains)
Amenities: None
Maximum grade: 26%
Cell service: Reliable

FINDING THE TRAILHEAD

The trailhead is located at the southeast corner of an unmarked parking area on U.S. 33 (Rawley Pike). There is no road signage, but there is a large trail kiosk in the parking area. **GPS:** N38°34'46.5" / W79°10'08.8"

THE CLIMB

It's hard to beat a hike to a historic fire tower, like the hike to High Knob Fire Tower near Harrisonburg. High Knob Fire Tower was completed in 1940 but was put out of commission in the early 1970s when this form of fire detection was deemed ineffective. A decision was made to retain High Knob Fire Tower as a visitor lookout tower. The structure on Shenandoah Mountain was named a National Historic Lookout in 1994 and was restored to its original appearance in 2003. After an easy 35-minute drive west of James Madison University, you can climb to big views in the morning, then explore the scenic campus in the afternoon.

This hike begins from an unmarked parking area on Rawley Pike (US 33), which is in West Virginia, but a mere stone's throw from the state line. The trail descends into the George Washington National Forest, just past a metal guardrail, meandering along to the fire tower, which straddles Virginia and West Virginia. Follow the yellow blazes that mark the Shenandoah Mountain Trail.

As you follow along an uneven ridgetop, you'll pass a primitive campsite at the 0.5-mile mark. Enjoy the views of surrounding mountains through leafless trees from fall to spring. A trail sign appears at the 0.8-mile mark. Turn left, but note that you are now hiking along the High Knob Trail, though the blazes are still yellow. This section is rocky and steep, but thankfully it is also short at just 0.1 mile. Turn right at the 0.9-mile mark onto a flat, private road.

◀ Top: The hike to High Knob Fire Tower begins on the yellow-blazed Shenandoah Mountain Trail.
Bottom: The High Knob Fire Tower sits on a ridge straddling Virginia and West Virginia

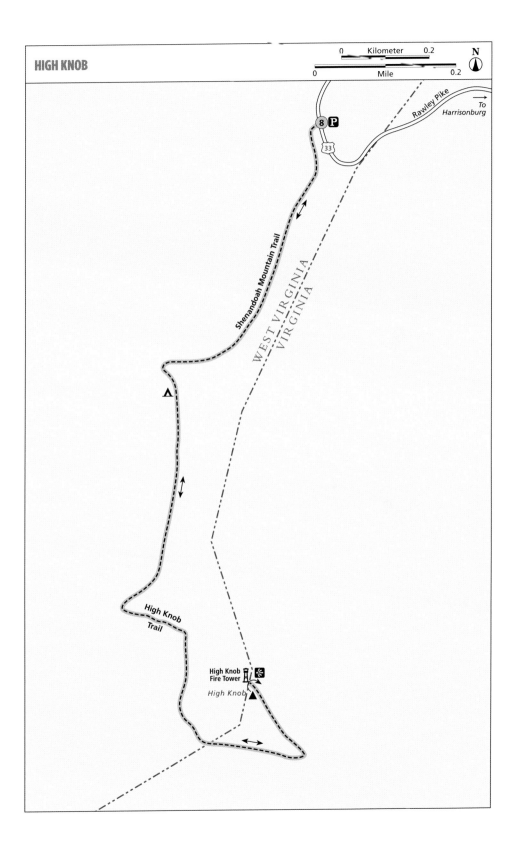

The wraparound catwalk at High Knob Fire Tower allows for 360-degree panoramas across the Blue Ridge Mountains.

Turn left for the final ascent at the 1.0-mile mark. The trail now skirts the edge of private property, so be respectful of the "Please Stay on the Trail" signs. Keep climbing and High Knob (elevation 4,107 feet) comes into view at the 1.3-mile mark. It's only a few steps farther to reach the historic stone fire tower. Admire the dramatic lookout tower from all angles before ascending thirty steps to walk the wraparound catwalk for sensational panoramas across the Blue Ridge Mountains. Once you've taken it all in, retrace your steps to the parking area. Your hike is complete at the 2.8-mile mark.

MILES AND DIRECTIONS

0.0 Begin from the southeast corner of the parking area on Rawley Pike. Descend into the forest by way of the yellow-blazed Shenandoah Mountain Trail.

0.8 Turn left onto the yellow-blazed High Knob Trail.

0.9 Turn right onto a flat, private road (still the High Knob Trail).

1.0 Veer left to continue on the High Knob Trail.

1.4 Arrive at High Knob Fire Tower. Retrace your steps to the parking area.

2.8 Arrive back at the parking area. Your hike is complete.

9 HIGHTOP MOUNTAIN

This short out-and-back hike along the Appalachian Trail leads to delightful 180-degree views from the Instagram-worthy rocky outcrop at Hightop Mountain.

Start: Parking area on Skyline Drive
Elevation gain: 912 feet
Distance: 3.0 miles out and back
Difficulty: Moderate
Hiking time: 1.5 to 2 hours
Best season: Year-round
Fees and permits: $$$$
Trail contact: Shenandoah National Park, 3655 Hwy. 211 E., Luray; (540) 999-3500; www.nps.gov/shen/
Dogs: Yes

Trail surface: Mostly dirt and rock trails
Land status: National park
Nearest town: Harrisonburg
Maps: National Geographic Trails Illustrated Topographic Map 228 (Shenandoah National Park); Map 11: AT in Shenandoah National Park (South District), PATC, Inc.
Amenities: None
Maximum grade: 19%
Cell service: Spotty

FINDING THE TRAILHEAD

The trailhead is located on the east side of Skyline Drive at milepost 66.7, a short 2 miles south of the park's Swift Run Gap entrance station.
GPS: N38°20'42.4" / W78°33'10.0"

THE CLIMB

At an elevation of 3,587 feet, Hightop Mountain is the highest point in the South District of Shenandoah National Park. It's also a fairly easy peak to reach, with a wide-open rocky outcrop that affords scenic views for miles. To be fair, the outcropping is slightly west of the true summit. The white-blazed Appalachian Trail neatly skirts around the peak, making it easier for thru-hikers, in particular, to continue on their way but also revel in big, big views.

The climb to the top of Hightop Mountain begins across Skyline Drive from the parking area. The trail location is important to note because the Appalachian Trail continues north from the back of the parking lot, but that path will not take you up Hightop Mountain. Cross over Skyline Drive and you will see a trail marker stamped with the AT symbol. From here, you will enter the forest as the gradual climb to the rocky outcrop begins at once.

The switchback-laden trail is well marked with the iconic white blazes. It's virtually impossible to get lost on your way to the top. It's not an especially scenic hike, but it is well shaded. At the 0.2-mile mark, you'll reach cool rock formations that are fun to climb on and make a nice break on the way to the peak. Press on, friends. The rocky outcrop is truly close at hand.

At the 1.4-mile mark, you'll see a short trail that leads off to the right. In summer, you will be greatly disappointed because the views are almost completely obscured by foliage. Thankfully, this is not the view for which you've been climbing. A much better view awaits.

Top: A well-shaded 1.5-mile hike along the white-blazed Appalachian Trail leads to a rocky overlook with far-reaching mountain views.

Bottom: At the 0.2-mile mark, you'll see large rocks on the side of the trail that are just right for a fun scramble before continuing on to the summit for big views.

Opposite page: Keep your eyes open for a partially obscured spur trail that leads to the scenic rocky outcrop at Hightop Mountain.

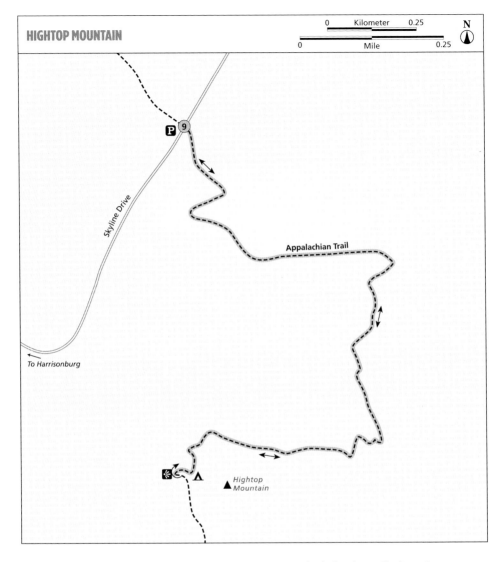

In a few more steps, you'll see a primitive campsite on the left. The well-cleared space is tucked away maybe 10 to 15 feet from the trail. There's space for at least one or two tents. This would be an outstanding spot to settle in for the night following a vibrantly colored sunset from the rocky viewpoint. Continue past the campsite, but keep your head on a swivel. In a few more steps, there's a small opening in the trees that leads to the overlook. It is *very* easy to miss, and you do *not* want to miss out on the mountain panoramas that go on for miles and miles. Settle in with a snack or rehydrate while taking in 180-degree west-facing views from atop Hightop Mountain that are simply spectacular. Once you've soaked them all up, retrace your steps to the parking lot.

Settle in and savor spectacular west-facing views across the Shenandoah Valley from the rocky overlook at Hightop Mountain.

MILES AND DIRECTIONS

0.0 Begin across Skyline Drive from the parking area at milepost 66.7. Follow the white-blazed Appalachian Trail.

1.4 Arrive at the first of two vistas. This one is almost entirely obscured in summer months. In a few more steps, there is a campsite to the left of the trail.

1.5 Arrive at the rocky overlook. Retrace your steps.

3.0 Arrive back at the parking area. Your hike is complete.

It's a short, steep hike to the jagged summit of Humpback Rocks near Waynesboro.

10 HUMPBACK ROCKS

This popular climb gets your heart pumping and rewards worthy hikers with spectacular views across the Rockfish and Shenandoah Valleys, even as far as Shenandoah National Park.

Start: Humpback Gap Overlook parking area
Elevation gain: 1,099 feet
Distance: 4.3-mile loop
Difficulty: Moderate
Hiking time: 2.5 to 4 hours
Best season: Year-round
Fees and permits: Free
Trail contact: George Washington and Jefferson National Forest (Glenwood-Pedlar Ranger District), 27 Ranger Ln., Natural Bridge Station; (540) 291-2188; www.fs.usda .gov/main/gwj

Dogs: Yes
Trail surface: Mostly dirt and gravel trails, some steps and rock scrambles
Land status: National forest
Nearest town: Waynesboro
Maps: National Geographic Trails Illustrated Topographic Map 791 (Staunton, Shenandoah Mountain)
Amenities: Porta-potties, picnic tables
Maximum grade: 30%
Cell service: Spotty

FINDING THE TRAILHEAD

 The trailhead is located at the front of the Humpback Gap Overlook parking area, which has a picnic table and six porta-potties. The lot is large, but it can fill quickly, especially during peak foliage season. **GPS:** N37°58'06.5" / W78°53'47.9"

THE CLIMB

The hike and scramble to reach the top of the jagged summit at Humpback Rocks (elevation 3,114 feet) is not for the faint of heart. However, this steep climb greatly rewards the determined few who take on the challenge. Situated in the George Washington National Forest near Waynesboro, Humpback Rocks is one of dozens of scenic hikes along the 469-mile Blue Ridge Parkway, which meanders across Virginia and North Carolina.

Humpback Rocks can be completed as a 2.0-mile out-and-back hike or as the described 4.3-mile loop hike. The counterclockwise loop hike includes downhill steps on the white-blazed Appalachian Trail on the return hike to the parking area. This forested section of trail features multiple switchbacks that make the descent less arduous than on the shorter out-and-back hike. Not only is the return hike more manageable, but you will see fewer hikers indulging in the scenic route on a northbound section of the Appalachian Trail on the way back to the parking area. Most visitors choose to hike up, then hike down.

From the parking area, look to the left of the porta-potties for a large trail kiosk with a map. The strenuous 700-foot climb to the summit begins just beyond the sign. Thankfully there are three or four benches on the way up the Humpback Rocks Trail. Everyone deserves to take a break from time to time, particularly before reaching the large wooden staircase at the 0.5-mile mark.

Take easy steps to reach the top of this staircase built into the trail on the way to Humpback Rocks.

At least two dozen steps stand between you and the top of this blue-blazed hiking trail. Well, a couple dozen steps plus some rock scrambles, a massive downed tree across the trail, then even more steps before the end of the Humpback Rocks Trail. There you'll see a trail sign indicating that Humpback Rocks is to the left, just 800 feet farther along the trail.

There are plenty of rocky outcrops to sit or stand on to revel in the sensational west-facing views across the Rockfish and Shenandoah Valleys. To the north, you can see as far as Shenandoah National Park. Once you soak in all the scenery, retrace your steps to the trail sign. Walk past this sign to continue on the Humpback Rocks Trail. This flat spur trail leads to the Appalachian Trail at the 1.3-mile mark. At the next trail sign, turn left

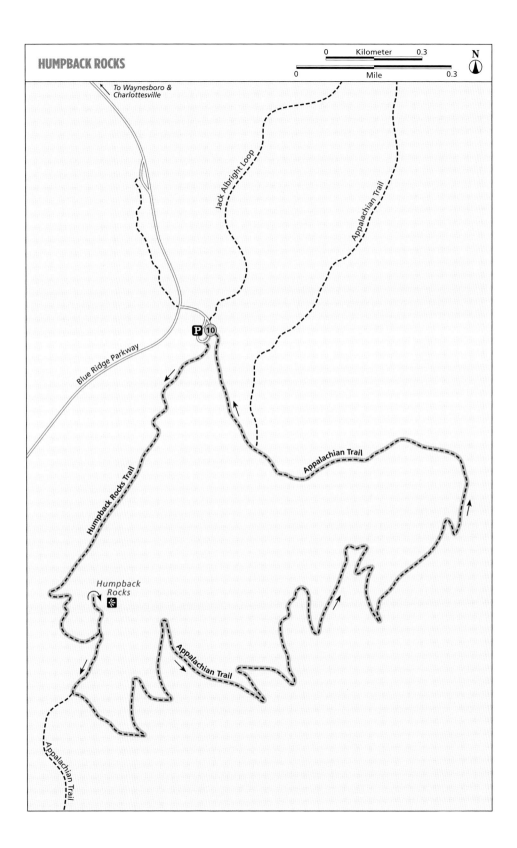

HUMPBACK ROCKS

N

0   Kilometer   0.3

0   Mile   0.3

To Waynesboro &
Charlottesville

Jack Albright Loop

Appalachian Trail

P 10

Blue Ridge Parkway

Humpback Rocks Trail

Appalachian Trail

Humpback
Rocks

Appalachian Trail

Appalachian Trail

onto the Appalachian Trail. You'll reach the first of a dozen switchbacks at the 1.5-mile mark. Trust us, these switchbacks make the descent to the parking area much easier on your knees. It's a less-trafficked section, which can be quiet and rather serene on a fair-weather afternoon.

At the 3.5-mile mark, stay left when the Appalachian Trail meets up with another trail. Then, at the 4.0-mile mark, stay left again to pick up the Jack Albright Loop. In less than 0.3 mile, you will arrive at the Humpback Gap Overlook parking area. Your hike is complete. If time allows, pop in the visitor center across the Blue Ridge Parkway at milepost 5.9. There's also a mountain life museum and a historic farm.

MILES AND DIRECTIONS

0.0 Begin at the front of the Humpback Gap Overlook parking area. Walk uphill on the Humpback Rocks Trail.

0.9 Arrive at a T-junction. Turn left onto the spur trail to Humpback Rocks. Retrace your steps to the T-junction.

1.1 Arrive at the T-junction. Continue straight ahead on the Humpback Rocks Trail.

1.3 Turn left onto the Appalachian Trail.

3.5 Arrive at a fork. Stay left for the Appalachian Trail.

4.0 Arrive at a fork. Stay left for the Jack Albright Loop.

4.3 Reach the parking area. Your hike is complete.

◀ Top: There are plenty of spots to take a seat and savor the views across the valley from atop Humpback Rocks.
Bottom: Humpback Rocks is a favorite hike in fall when surrounding foliage is bursting with ambers, golds, and fiery oranges.

11 LEWIS PEAK

This lesser-known summit hike in Shenandoah National Park's South District wows with inspiring mountain views and contemplative stretches across several different trails.

Start: Browns Gap parking area
Elevation gain: 1,857 feet
Distance: 9.3 miles out and back
Difficulty: Moderate
Hiking time: 4 to 5 hours
Best season: Year-round
Fees and permits: $$$$
Trail contact: Shenandoah National Park, 3655 Hwy. 211 E., Luray; (540) 999-3500; www.nps.gov/shen/
Dogs: Yes

Trail surface: Mostly dirt and rock trails
Land status: National park
Nearest town: Waynesboro
Maps: National Geographic Trails Illustrated Topographic Map 228 (Shenandoah National Park); Map 11: AT in Shenandoah National Park (South District), PATC, Inc.
Amenities: None
Maximum grade: 17%
Cell service: Fairly reliable

FINDING THE TRAILHEAD

The trailhead is located in the Browns Gap parking area at milepost 83 on Skyline Drive. There's room for about a dozen cars to park and also a comfortable space for an RV. **GPS:** N38°14'26.5" / W78°42'39.3"

THE CLIMB

Located in Shenandoah National Park, Lewis Peak (elevation 2,704 feet) isn't as well known or as well trafficked as other summit hikes in the park's South District, like Blackrock Summit and Hightop Mountain, but it's a peak worthy of a place on your must-hike list. It's a quiet out-and-back hike with a gradual ascent that leads to big northwest-facing views.

From the parking lot, the hike begins at the concrete trail marker that guides hikers onto a northbound stretch of the white-blazed Appalachian Trail. You'll be on this iconic trail for only 0.5 mile before turning left onto the blue-blazed Big Run Loop Trail. Mind your footing (and your ankles); much of the hike is on trails that hug the mountain, with a steep ascent and descent on either side.

Get ready to step foot on a new trail at the 1.2-mile mark as you continue straight ahead for the blue-blazed Rockytop Trail (the Big Run Loop Trail leads off to the right). When you reach a fork at the 1.6-mile mark, stay right to continue on the Rockytop Trail. This trail is going to live up to its name, too. As in, rocky. You'll even pass through a talus slope (essentially, a massive rockslide) at the 2.4-mile mark and then a second one shortly after. Both are very manageable, but pay attention to avoid an unwanted twist or sprain.

Top: The hike to Lewis Peak begins with a short stretch along a northbound section of ▶ the white-blazed Appalachian Trail.

Bottom: You'll reach the first of two rocky talus slopes at the 2.4-mile mark. Watch your step and mind your footing as you hike across this section of the Rockytop Trail.

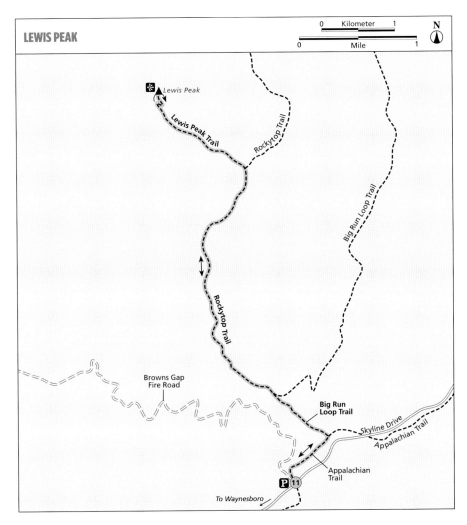

At the 3.6-mile mark, you'll change trails one more time as you approach yet another fork in the trail. This time, stay left for the Lewis Peak Trail, which descends for the next 0.5 mile. Don't move too quickly in your haste to reach Lewis Peak. The best view of the hike comes up on the right at the 3.8-mile mark. You'll need to take a few steps off the trail onto a talus slope, but you will be awed by the spectacular views toward Massanutten Mountain. The final ascent to Lewis Peak begins at the 4.2-mile mark. You'll need to dig deep as you encounter several switchbacks, but you'll also be rewarded with inspiring mountain views in all directions as you climb. You'll reach a concrete trail marker at the 4.4-mile mark, but stay right to continue your ascent.

You arrive at the summit of Lewis Peak at the 4.7-mile mark. It's an open rock face, so go ahead and take a seat to savor the far-reaching views. The trail dead-ends at this overlook, so simply retrace your steps to the parking area once you've soaked in all the sensational vistas.

At the 3.8-mile mark, prepare to reap serious rewards as you reach a wide-open vista with fantastic northwest-facing views toward Massanutten Mountain.

The Lewis Peak Trail dead-ends at the open-face summit of Lewis Peak. Sit and soak up the mountain views before retracing your steps to the Browns Gap parking area.

MILES AND DIRECTIONS

0.0 Begin at the concrete marker in the Browns Gap parking area. Your first steps are on the Appalachian Trail.

0.5 Turn left onto the blue-blazed Big Run Loop Trail.

1.2 Continue straight ahead for the blue-blazed Rockytop Trail.

1.6 Veer right to stay on the Rockytop Trail.

2.4 Reach the first of two talus slopes on the trail.

3.6 Stay left for the blue-blazed Lewis Peak Trail.

3.8 Arrive at a big mountain view on the right side of the trail.

4.4 Stay right when you reach a concrete trail marker.

4.7 Reach the open-face summit of Lewis Peak. Retrace your steps to the parking area.

9.3 Arrive back at the parking area. Your hike is complete.

12 MARY'S ROCK

Revel in far-reaching views on a clear day from the summit of Mary's Rock. On the way up, make stops for a sparkling stream and an old stone chimney, which is all that remains of a homestead cabin from the 1940s.

Start: Meadow Spring parking area
Elevation gain: 669 feet
Distance: 2.8 miles out and back
Difficulty: Moderate
Hiking time: 1.5 to 2 hours
Best season: Year-round
Fees and permits: $$$$
Trail contact: Shenandoah National Park, 3655 Hwy. 211 E., Luray; (540) 999-3500; www.nps.gov/shen/
Dogs: Yes
Trail surface: Mostly rock and dirt trails

Land status: National park
Nearest town: Sperryville (east) or Luray (west)
Maps: National Geographic Trails Illustrated Topographic Map 228 (Shenandoah National Park); Map 10: AT in Shenandoah National Park (Central District), PATC, Inc.
Amenities: None
Maximum grade: 22%
Cell service: Spotty

FINDING THE TRAILHEAD

The trailhead is located across Skyline Drive from the Meadow Spring parking area at milepost 33.5. Arrive early to get a space in the lot; there are just twelve parking spots for this popular summit hike. **GPS:** N38°38'17.3" / W78°18'50.3"

THE CLIMB

There are two routes that lead hikers to the top of Mary's Rock for spectacular vistas. This one approaches the summit from the south and clocks in at 1.0 mile less than the approach from the north. The trail marker is easy to find, but note that it's on the opposite side of Skyline Drive from the parking area. You'll see a trail marker at the south end of the parking area, but that one marks the start of the Buck Hollow and Hazel Mountain Trails.

This hike begins with a short stretch along the blue-blazed Meadow Spring Trail. Wooden steps built into the trail make the climb more manageable. At the 0.4-mile mark, take time to check out the crumbling stone chimney from a mountain cabin that burned to the ground in the 1940s. The chimney is all that remains of a former home inhabited by one of more than 450 families that lived within the boundaries of the national park in the 1930s and 1940s. At this spot, you are also steps from the hiking trail's namesake spring.

At the 0.7-mile mark, turn right onto the white-blazed Appalachian Trail. From here, you'll walk this iconic trail to the 1.3-mile mark, at which point the two routes to the top of Mary's Rock converge. Turn left onto a blue-blazed spur trail for the final steps to reach Mary's Rock.

As the trees and greenery open up at the summit, prepare to be awed by the wildly scenic views from Mary's Rock at the 1.4-mile mark. Stare out into the Shenandoah

A crumbling stone chimney is all that remains of a mountain cabin that was once inhabited by one of more than 450 families living within the boundaries of the national park.

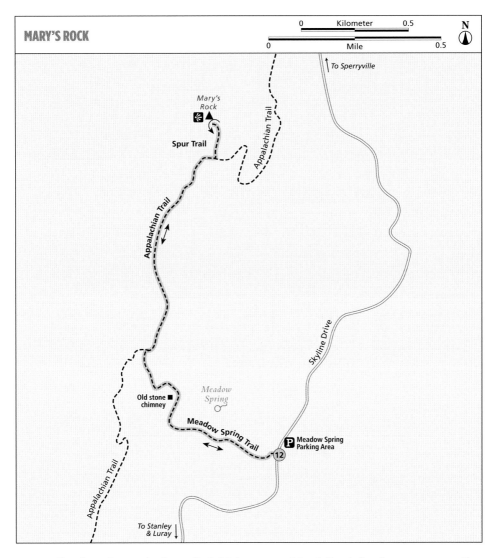

Valley from the overlook or climb high up onto Mary's Rock for the most outstanding panoramas, including the northern section of Shenandoah National Park.

Retrace your steps to the parking area. Pay attention since the spur trail ends after just 0.1 mile. Turn right for the southbound section of the Appalachian Trail, which will guide you back to the parking area. The alternate path to the left leads to the Panorama parking lot for those who opted for the northern approach trail to Mary's Rock.

MILES AND DIRECTIONS

0.0 Begin across Skyline Drive from the Meadow Spring parking area.

0.4 Note the chimney and former homestead on the left.

0.7 Turn right onto the Appalachian Trail.

The iconic white-blazed Appalachian Trail leads hikers coming from the north and south to the top of Mary's Rock.

1.3	Turn left onto a blue-blazed spur trail for the final ascent to Mary's Rock.
1.4	Reach Mary's Rock. Retrace your steps to the parking area.
2.8	Arrive back at the parking area. Your hike is complete.

OPTION

For a longer hike, arrive at Mary's Rock by way of the northern approach. This 3.4-mile out-and-back trail begins at the back of the very large Panorama parking area at milepost 31.6 on Skyline Drive. The trail is a bit longer and steeper but equally impressive with outstanding views from the craggy summit. This is a great option if you find there are no available spaces at the Meadow Spring parking area. You'll also find restrooms at the Panorama parking area.

Get ready to be awed as you reach the summit of Mary's Rock. Scramble up high on the rock for even more outstanding vistas across the Shenandoah Valley.

13 MOUNT PLEASANT

Get ready to be awed by east- and west-facing overlooks from the top of Mount Pleasant. The west overlook wows with otherworldly sunsets.

Start: Mount Pleasant National Scenic Area parking area
Elevation gain: 1,306 feet
Distance: 6.5-mile lollipop
Difficulty: Moderate
Hiking time: 4 to 5 hours
Best season: Mar–Nov (due to passability of Wiggins Spring Road)
Fees and permits: Free
Trail contact: George Washington and Jefferson National Forest (Glenwood-Pedlar Ranger District), 27 Ranger Ln., Natural Bridge

Station; (540) 291-2188; www.fs.usda.gov/detail/gwj
Dogs: Yes, on leash no longer than 6 feet
Trail surface: Mostly dirt and gravel trails
Land status: National forest
Nearest town: Lexington
Maps: National Geographic Trails Illustrated Topographic Map 789 (Lexington, Blue Ridge Mountains)
Amenities: None
Maximum grade: 14%
Cell service: Spotty

FINDING THE TRAILHEAD

The trailhead is located adjacent to the parking area at the end of Wiggins Spring Road. Follow the signs for the Mount Pleasant National Scenic Area. You'll pass parking on the left for the Cole Mountain hike, then stay right in another 0.1 mile when you see the sign for the trailhead. The lot is not big and not organized, so park where you can and be considerate of others planning to park, too. **GPS:** N37°45'31.9" / W79°11'18.8"

THE CLIMB

The name alone—Mount Pleasant—conjures up so much happiness and positivity that you'll have to add this hike near Buena Vista to your must-do list. Make it a sunset hike, too. The vibrant colors across the mountains will not disappoint. You'll be so glad you checked off this summit hike in Virginia.

The loop hike begins from the parking area at the end of Wiggins Spring Road. Look for the sign for the Henry Lanum Loop Trail. From the sign you'll note that it's nearly the same distance to the summit whether you start on the trail to the right or the left. For this hike, begin on the right-most trail for a counterclockwise hike. From here, it's 2.75 miles to the summit of Mount Pleasant (elevation 4,013 feet). You've got this one.

The trail starts out fairly flat. In the first mile, you'll gain just 23 feet in elevation. Easy-peasy. You'll then cross over a modest creek at the 1.2-mile mark, but this marks the beginning of the ascent on this blue-blazed trail. It gets rocky, too. At the 2.2-mile mark, you'll see a sign indicating that the summit is a mere 0.5 mile farther up the trail. This spur trail to the summit is the Mount Pleasant Trail. At this junction, you'll also

◀ Top: The hike to the top of Mount Pleasant starts out flat but becomes much more rocky as you climb starting at the 1.2-mile mark.

Bottom: You will not be disappointed by a sunset from the west overlook of Mount Pleasant.

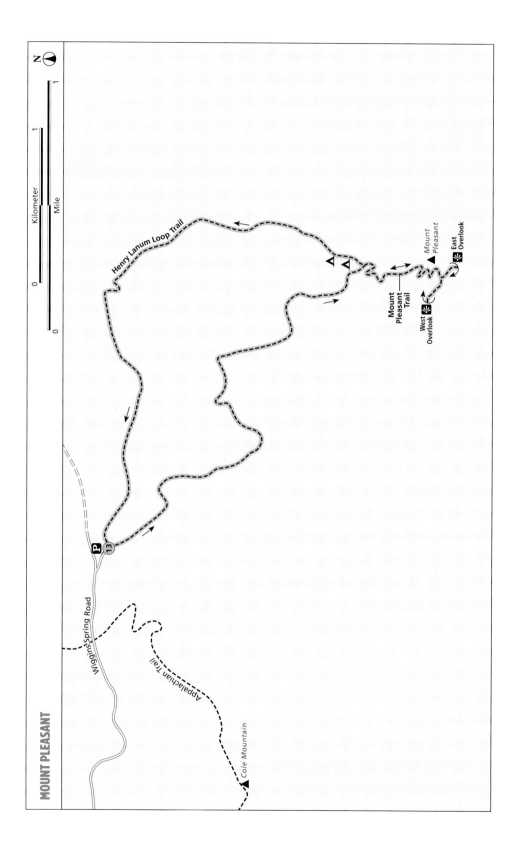

MOUNT PLEASANT

N

Kilometer

Mile

Henry Lanum Loop Trail

Wiggins Spring Road

Appalachian Trail

Cole Mountain

P
13

Mount
Pleasant
Trail

West
Overlook

Mount
Pleasant

East
Overlook

The mountains seem to go on forever as you take in the views from the east overlook.

see an open area for tent camping. It's large enough for a few families to set up tents at this camp spot.

Turn right at the sign and continue ascending, now on a switchback-laden path to the top. You have two options at the 2.8-mile mark. There are two different overlooks: Mount Pleasant East and Mount Pleasant West. You'll want to check out both to see which view you like better (spoiler: both are amazing). Each rocky overlook is just 0.1 mile from this east-west midpoint with the sign. As you can imagine, the west side definitely wows with the more sensational sunset. However, if you opt to backpack up and stay the night, look to the east side for more spots to set up your tent. There's also a stone fire ring and several logs to use as benches.

Once you've ogled the views at each overlook, retrace your steps along the switch-backed spur trail until you return to the Henry Lanum Loop Trail at the 4.1-mile mark. Stay right at the trail sign to complete the loop. The last 2.4 miles of this hike are not all downhill. It's down, then up, then down, then up, then down one final time for the last 0.7 mile to the parking area. At the 6.5-mile mark, your hike is complete.

MILES AND DIRECTIONS

0.0 Begin this counterclockwise loop hike from the right-most trailhead for the Henry Lanum Loop Trail, adjacent to the parking area.

1.2 Cross over a small creek.

2.2 Turn right at the sign onto the Mount Pleasant Trail.

2.8 Arrive at a directional sign for the West Overlook and East Overlook. Explore both rocky overlooks, then retrace your steps along the Mount Pleasant Trail.

4.1 Turn right at the Henry Lanum Loop Trail.

6.5 Arrive back at the parking area. Your hike is complete.

14 OLD RAG

Get ready for rock scrambles across large boulders and big views from atop Old Rag Mountain at Shenandoah National Park as you check off this bucket-list hike.

Start: Lot one on Nethers Road
Elevation gain: 2,608 feet
Distance: 9.8-mile lollipop
Difficulty: Strenuous
Hiking time: 6 to 7 hours
Best season: Year-round
Fees and permits: $$$$
Trail contact: Shenandoah National Park, 3655 Hwy. 211 E., Luray; (540) 999-3500; www.nps.gov/shen/
Dogs: No
Trail surface: Mostly dirt and gravel trails

Land status: National park
Nearest town: Sperryville
Maps: National Geographic Trails Illustrated Topographic Map 228 (Shenandoah National Park); Map 10: AT in Shenandoah National Park (Central District), PATC, Inc.
Amenities: Vault toilets
Maximum grade: 30%
Cell service: None
Special considerations: This hike is not considered safe in wet, snowy, or icy conditions.

FINDING THE TRAILHEAD

The trailhead is located to the left of the ranger station at the back of lot one on Nethers Road. **GPS:** N38°34'19.8" / W78°17'38.1"

THE CLIMB

Old Rag is widely considered the most popular hike in Virginia. It's on more bucket lists than you can count. It was even ranked among the best hikes in the world by *Outside* magazine. It's so feted (translation: over-visited), in fact, that a pilot day-hiking ticket program was put in place from March 1 to November 30, 2022, to help ease crowding by limiting the number of hikers on Old Rag Mountain (elevation 3,274 feet). The program set a cap of 800 hikers per day, and required each hiker to make a reservation at www.recreation.gov for a specific day and pay a $1 fee—in addition to the park entrance fee.

From the parking area, walk past the large trail kiosk on your right and across the footbridge. From here, the ascent begins along the switchback-laden Ridge Trail, which skirts on and off private property for 0.8 mile. You'll then reach a concrete trail marker at a fork in the forested trail. Stay left to continue climbing the blue-blazed Ridge Trail.

The Old Rag hike is well known for its tricky rock scramble as you close in on the summit. However, for those not keen on a scramble that requires all limbs to successfully navigate, you can revel in big, wide-open views at the 2.6-mile mark. Here you'll reach a rocky outcrop that's easy to access for spectacular south-facing vistas.

The rock scramble begins in earnest at the 2.8-mile mark. From this point on, it's a full mile of pulling, gripping, scrambling, and climbing to reach the summit. That noted, take

◄ Top: For those less or not at all inclined to navigate a solid mile of rock scrambles, you can enjoy big views from a rocky outcrop at the 2.6-mile mark.

Bottom: On the way down from the top of Old Rag, pause at Byrd's Nest Shelter, one of two stone day-use shelters on the west side of the craggy mountain.

One of the highlights of the Old Rag hike is the stair steps built into and through one of the large boulders near the top of the mountain.

your time. It's not a race. Let's give Search and Rescue (SAR) a break today. Be prepared to navigate rocky passages, strategize tight spaces, shimmy along flat, granite surfaces, and summon all your strength to hoist yourself up onto boulders and large rocks. It's both exhausting and exhilarating.

Early on in the rock scramble, you'll reach a narrow crevasse that's 6 or 7 feet deep. You've got to find your footing and get down into it to continue on. It helps to have a fellow hiker in front of you to guide you into the crevasse. Take a deep breath once you've completed this section, then keep scrambling. At the 3.0-mile mark, you will reach a set of steps that goes right through a large boulder. Then, at the 3.8-mile mark, you'll see a sign for the summit.

Turn right here, then get ready to take in the views from all vantage points. There's lots of space to sit, snack, and savor all the far-reaching mountain vistas. This is quite an accomplishment, so take your time and soak it all in.

From here, retrace your steps to the trail sign, then turn right to begin descending Old Rag. Pause at Byrd's Nest Shelter at the 4.5-mile mark. This is a day-use shelter with a picnic table. Turn right to connect with the blue-blazed Saddle Trail.

At the 5.4-mile mark, you'll reach the Old Rag Shelter, another day-use shelter with a picnic table. There is also a vault toilet. Turn right at the large trail kiosk (Post Office Junction) for the yellow-blazed gravel Weakley Hollow Fire Road at the 6.0-mile mark. Some hikers find this section to be ho-hum, but it's a welcome break from the strenuous

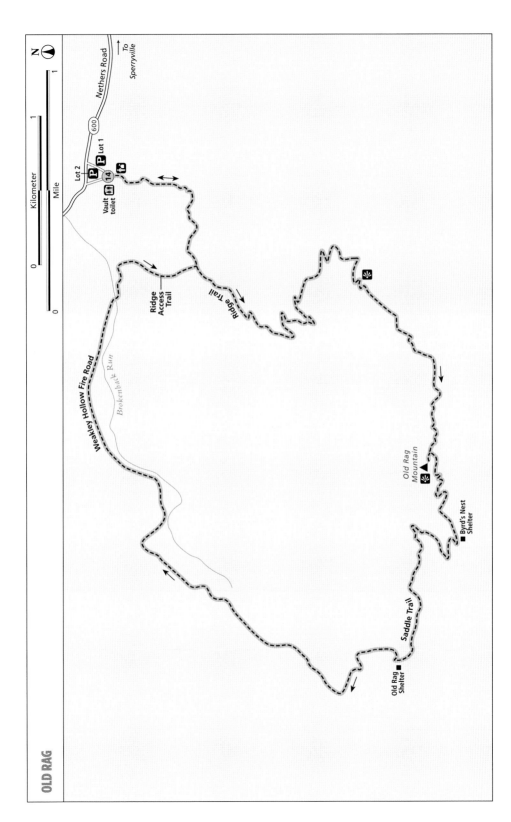

OLD RAG

N

To Sperryville

Nethers Road

600

Lot 1

Lot 2

14

Vault toilet

Kilometer

Mile

Ridge Access Trail

Ridge Trail

Weakley Hollow Fire Road

Brokenback Run

Old Rag Mountain

Byrd's Nest Shelter

Saddle Trail

Old Rag Shelter

Take your time as you take in all the wide-open views from the summit of Old Rag Mountain. You've earned them.

rock scramble. It's also a nice opportunity to reflect on your accomplishment before returning to the parking area.

At the 7.3-mile mark, you'll cross over Brokenback Run, then walk with the cascading waters on your right for the next mile. At the 8.3-mile mark, you'll cross over Brokenback Run a few more times by way of four different footbridges. Turn right onto the Ridge Access Trail at the 8.6-mile mark, then close the loop at the 9.0-mile mark. Turn left here onto the Ridge Trail for the final steps to the parking area. Your hike is complete at the 9.8-mile mark.

MILES AND DIRECTIONS

0.0 Begin on the Ridge Trail, to the left of the ranger station at the back of lot one.

0.8 Reach a fork in the trail. Stay left to continue on the blue-blazed Ridge Trail.

2.6 Arrive at a rocky outcrop for big views.

2.8 Reach the rock scramble to the top of Old Rag.

3.8 Arrive at a trail sign. Turn right for the summit of Old Rag. When ready, retrace your steps to the sign, then turn right to begin to descend Old Rag.

4.5 Reach Byrd's Nest Shelter. Turn right on the blue-blazed Saddle Trail.

5.4 Arrive at Old Rag Shelter.

6.0 Turn right at the large trail kiosk for the yellow-blazed Weakley Hollow Fire Road.

8.6 Turn right on the Ridge Access Trail.

9.0 Turn left on the Ridge Trail.

9.8 Arrive back at the parking area. Your hike is complete.

15 THE PRIEST

This wooded hike challenges with an unrelenting climb, but your expectations will be exceeded when you arrive at the summit of The Priest for plenty of eye-pleasing mountain vistas.

Start: Parking area on VA 56
Elevation gain: 3,169 feet
Distance: 9.0 miles out and back
Difficulty: Strenuous
Hiking time: 7 to 8 hours
Best season: Year-round
Fees and permits: Free
Trail contact: George Washington and Jefferson National Forest (Glenwood-Pedlar Ranger District), 27 Ranger Ln., Natural Bridge Station; (540) 291-2188; www.fs.usda .gov/detail/gwj

Dogs: Yes
Trail surface: Mostly dirt and rock trails
Land status: National forest
Nearest town: Buena Vista
Maps: National Geographic Trails Illustrated Topographic Map 791 (Staunton, Shenandoah Mountain)
Amenities: None
Maximum grade: 27%
Cell service: Fairly reliable

FINDING THE TRAILHEAD

The trailhead is located at the parking area on VA 56 (Crabtree Falls Highway). **GPS:** N37°50'18.5" / W79°01'23.5"

THE CLIMB

The Priest has quite a reputation among hikers, and let's just say, it's less than holy. You may have more than a few unkind words for this mountain as you engage in an absolutely unrelenting climb, crushed by an elevation gain of more than 3,100 feet over the course of the 4.5-mile ascent to the summit. The Priest is so famous (maybe infamous) in Virginia that you can buy an iron-on patch at www.virginiabackpacking.com that reads "Seek Forgiveness," presumably for all the naughty words you've uttered on your way to the top.

The hike to the summit of The Priest is entirely along a southbound stretch of the Appalachian Trail. The trail sets off into the George Washington and Jefferson National Forest from the northwest corner of the small parking lot. From the get-go, you're slowly ascending as Cripple Creek politely burbles on the left side of the trail.

At the 1.3-mile mark, stay alert. You'll cross over Cripple Creek, but if you're not paying attention, you'll continue on what is essentially a social trail that has been inadvertently created by other hikers not paying attention. Instead, you need to take a sharp left turn at a switchback to stay on the Appalachian Trail. Speaking of switchbacks, you will encounter more than twenty switchbacks on the way to the summit, which presumably is a better option than hiking straight up the mountain. You'll encounter all of the switchbacks over a 2-mile section of the hike—from the 1.3-mile mark to the 3.3-mile mark. Just take it slow and steady.

Your efforts will be rewarded early on, too. At the 2.7-mile mark, there's a large rocky outcrop with gorgeous wide-open, southeast-facing views of mountains, open green

The climb to the top of The Priest feels unrelenting at times, but the eye-pleasing views at the top make it worth all your efforts.

Savor views of mountains, working farms, and fruit orchards from a rocky overlook on the way to the summit.

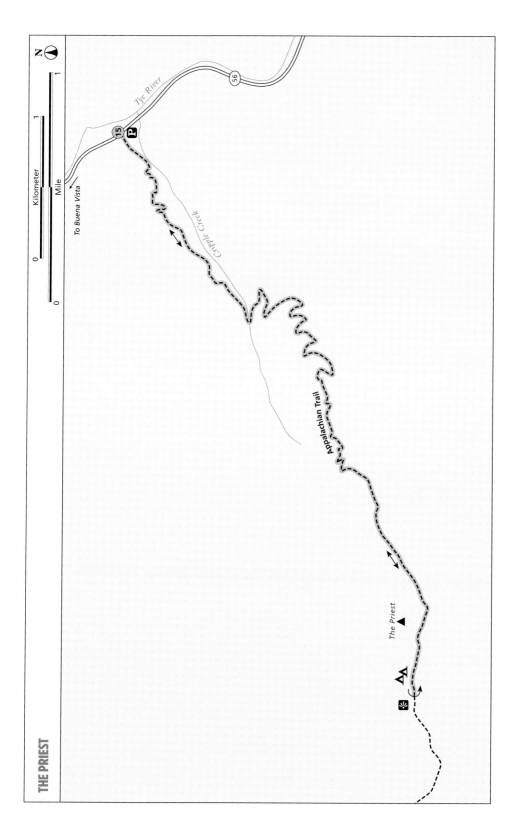

THE PRIEST

N

To Buena Vista

Tye River

56

15

P

Cripple Creek

Appalachian Trail

The Priest

Kilometer

Mile

Hold onto your hat when you reach the top of The Priest. You may be blown away by both wind gusts and bold mountain vistas.

spaces, and fruit orchards. It's the absolute perfect spot to stop for a much-deserved snack and hydration break, but don't settle in for too long; more views are to come, but also more elevation.

At this point the hikers in your party may become very quiet. For the next 0.4 mile, the trail is especially steep with a grade that runs from 20 to 25 percent. It's tough, but it's one of just a few very steep sections on the way to the top. The trail then levels out at the 4.1-mile mark. It's very flat. You may begin to worry that you've missed the summit. Wait, where are the views? Stay calm.

At the 4.5-mile mark, a spur trail leads to nice views, but don't be fooled. This is a false summit. There are better views, and they are literally just a few steps farther. Once you arrive, you will know you have arrived because the views from atop the large boulders at the summit are beyond sensational. You'll see several primitive campsites at the top, too. It can get very windy at the top. It's also much chillier at the summit than it is at the trailhead, so pack an extra layer in your daypack. Once you've soaked it all in, retrace your steps to the parking area, filled with the memories of the climb and the wildly eye-pleasing vistas that were so worth the journey.

MILES AND DIRECTIONS

0.0   Begin at the parking lot on VA 56 (Crabtree Falls Highway).

1.3   Cross Cripple Creek, then make a sharp left at a switchback turn.

2.7   Arrive at a rocky outcrop with wide-open views.

4.5   Reach the summit of The Priest. Retrace your steps to the parking area.

9.0   Arrive back at the trailhead. Your hike is complete.

The far-reaching mountain views from the summit of The Priest are sensational, especially in the fall when the landscape is draped in fiery orange and golden yellow.

16 ROBERTSON MOUNTAIN

The hike to the top of Robertson Mountain may share a parking lot with Old Rag Mountain, one of the most popular hikes in Virginia, but this summit hike is no less exceptional.

Start: Lot one on Nethers Road
Elevation gain: 2,444 feet
Distance: 9.7-mile lollipop
Difficulty: Strenuous
Hiking time: 6 to 7 hours
Best season: Year-round
Fees and permits: $$$$
Trail contact: Shenandoah National Park, 3655 Hwy. 211 E., Luray; (540) 999-3500; www.nps.gov/shen/
Dogs: Yes
Trail surface: Mostly dirt and gravel trails

Land status: National park
Nearest town: Sperryville
Maps: National Geographic Trails Illustrated Topographic Map 228 (Shenandoah National Park); Map 10: AT in Shenandoah National Park (Central District), PATC, Inc.
Amenities: Vault toilets
Maximum grade: 28%
Cell service: Spotty (only available at the summit)

FINDING THE TRAILHEAD

The trailhead is located to the right of the ranger station at the front of lot one on Nethers Road. **GPS:** N38°34'17.5" / W78°17'39.0"

THE CLIMB

Robertson Mountain (elevation 3,297 feet) is one of the less-frequented sister mountains to wildly popular Old Rag Mountain. The two are so close that they share a parking lot. However, don't let the crowds and the fact that Old Rag now requires a permit for a day hike make you think Robertson Mountain is an also-ran hike. In fact, it's pretty awesome all on its own.

At the front of the main parking area (lot one), there is a small ranger station where you'll pay the entrance free to the national park. From here, turn right for the Robertson Mountain hike. A wide gravel path leads hikers across a pedestrian footbridge, then alongside lot two, which is for horse trailers and RVs (it's also an overflow lot for cars). At the 0.1-mile mark, turn left onto a paved road (Nethers Road). This leads to the Weakley Hollow Fire Road at the 0.5-mile mark. Get ready to cross bridges three or four times over gently flowing Brokenback Run. It's a very manageable ascent along the wide fire road.

You'll cross over Brokenback Run one more time, then pass the Corbin Hollow Trail, before you reach a concrete trail marker on the right at the 1.8-mile mark. Turn right here for the blue-blazed Robertson Mountain Trail. Here the trail narrows and the real fun begins. As in, real, heart-pumping elevation as you climb to the overlook atop Robertson Mountain. You may feel at some points that the ascent is both unrelenting and

◀ Top: Take in the views of burbling Brokenback Run as you hike along the Weakley Hollow Fire Road.

Bottom: The ascent up the blue-blazed Robertson Mountain Trail will feel unrelenting at times, but your efforts will be rewarded when you reach the rocky overlook at the summit.

This hike ends with more than 5 miles of walking along wide, gravel fire roads, but for many it's a welcome respite from the challenging climb to the top of Robertson Mountain.

never-ending. Take your time, stop when you need to catch your breath, and rehydrate often, especially when tackling this hike in warm-weather months. Your best bet may be to hike Robertson Mountain between late fall and early spring when you can savor the vistas of surrounding mountains through leafless trees.

At the 3.5-mile mark, you will reach a very nice overlook on the right, but the views are really only visible when the trees are not full of foliage. However, the summit is very close, only another 0.2 mile from this rocky ledge. At the 3.6-mile mark, you will arrive at a fork in the trail that is not marked, but you want to turn left for the west-facing summit views, including views of Hawksbill Mountain (elevation 4,051 feet), the tallest peak at Shenandoah National Park. From here, it's a very short walk to views that are worth every ounce of your efforts to climb this mountain. Note, however, that it can be much colder at the rocky overlook than in the parking lot. Plan accordingly.

After you soak in all the views, retrace your steps to the fork and turn left to continue on the Robertson Mountain Trail. At the 4.4-mile mark, the trail dead-ends at the yellow-blazed Old Rag Fire Road. Turn left here to continue on this lollipop hike. You'll see a large sign on the left directing hikers to parking for Old Rag by way of the Weakley Hollow Fire Road. Turn left here to continue the slow, gradual descent along the gravel fire road. You'll close the loop at the 7.8-mile mark. Turn right to stay on the Weakley Hollow Fire Road. Some people find the lengthy walk of more than 5 miles on forested fire road to be rather boring, but many also find it a welcome break after the challenging

ROBERTSON MOUNTAIN

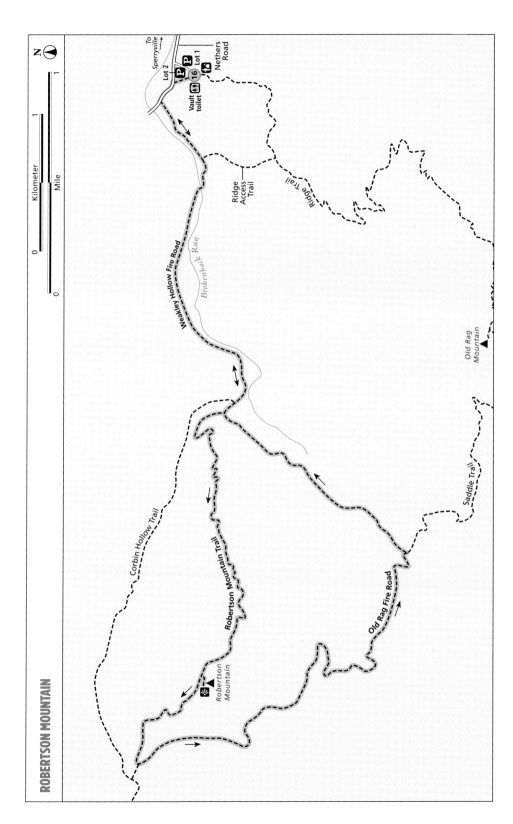

West-facing views from Robertson Mountain allow hikers to see across Shenandoah National Park, including Hawskbill Summit, the national park's highest peak.

climb to the summit of Robertson Mountain. Once on the Weakley Hollow Fire Road, retrace your steps to the parking area. Your summit hike is complete at the 9.7–mile mark.

MILES AND DIRECTIONS

0.0 Begin at the ranger station at the front of lot one on Nethers Road. Turn right to begin walking on a wide gravel path that runs in front of lot two.

0.1 Turn left onto a paved road (Nethers Road).

0.5 Continue on the gravel Weakley Hollow Fire Road.

1.8 Turn right for the blue-blazed Robertson Mountain Trail.

3.5 Arrive at a rocky overlook on the right (views largely visible in winter).

3.6 Reach a fork in the trail. Turn left onto a spur trail.

3.7 Arrive at the overlook for Robertson Mountain. Retrace your steps on the spur trail, then turn left on the Robertson Mountain Trail.

4.4 Turn left on the yellow-blazed Old Rag Fire Road.

6.7 Turn left onto the Weakley Hollow Fire Road.

7.8 Turn right to continue on the Weakley Hollow Fire Road, then retrace your steps to the main parking area.

9.7 Arrive back at the parking area. Your hike is complete.

17 SPY ROCK

A forested hike, including steps on the white-blazed Appalachian Trail, leads to 360-degree panoramas from atop a granite dome, Spy Rock.

Start: Gate on Meadows Lane with "Foot Travel Welcome" sign
Elevation gain: 1,270 feet
Distance: 5.8 miles out and back
Difficulty: Moderate
Hiking time: 3 to 4 hours
Best season: Year-round
Fees and permits: Free
Trail contact: George Washington and Jefferson National Forest (Glenwood-Pedlar Ranger District), 27 Ranger Ln., Natural Bridge Station; (540) 291-2188; www.fs.usda .gov/detail/gwj
Dogs: Yes

Trail surface: Mostly dirt and rock trails
Land status: National forest
Nearest town: Pembroke
Maps: National Geographic Trails Illustrated Topographic Map 791 (Staunton, Shenandoah Mountain)
Amenities: Vault toilet at Crabtree Meadows parking area
Maximum grade: 21%
Cell service: Spotty
Special considerations: The 3.2-mile gravel road leading to the parking area is bumpy and not well-suited for sedans. A four-wheel-drive vehicle is recommended.

FINDING THE TRAILHEAD

The trailhead is located on Meadows Lane, at the gate with the "Foot Travel Welcome" sign. There's a primitive campsite and room for maybe three cars to park along the road. If you get shut out here, continue on another 0.6 mile to the Crabtree Meadows parking lot. Here you'll find room for at least fifteen to twenty cars and a vault toilet at the front of the lot, but you'll need to walk 0.6 mile back up the gravel road to the trailhead. **GPS:** N37°49'52.9" / W79°05'34.5"

THE CLIMB

Thanks to an elevation gain of 1,270 feet over the course of a nearly 3.0-mile trek to the top of Spy Rock, this hike is firmly positioned in the moderate category. It may be a toss-up, however, when it comes to the greater challenge: climbing Spy Rock or parking to hike Spy Rock. Not just parking, but navigating the gravel Meadows Lane to reach the trailhead. From the get-go, a sign warns that the road is only for four-wheel-drive vehicles. Take it slow since you'll encounter two stream crossings on the way.

The hike begins along an unnamed connector trail that is sometimes referred to as the Spy Rock Trail. This blue-blazed trail starts on a gravel service road with a closed metal gate and a "Foot Travel Welcome" sign. You'll see a primitive campsite on the left as you start to hike. At the 0.5-mile mark, you will arrive at a trail sign. Turn right for the southbound section of the Appalachian Trail to Spy Rock. It's essentially a hairpin turn. White blazes lead you on a mild ascent through the George Washington and Jefferson National Forest. Spy Rock is the big prize, but there are a few small rewards on this hike, including wide-open south-facing views that can be savored from the trail at the 1.8-mile mark.

SPY ROCK

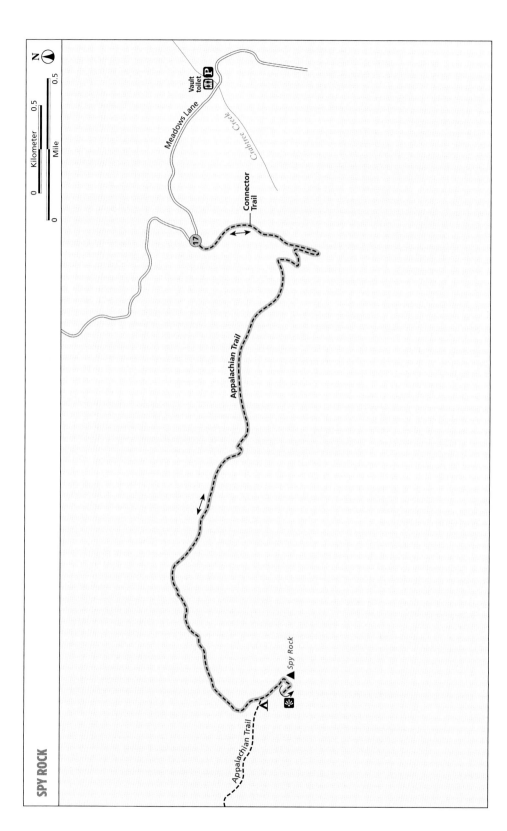

At the 1.8-mile mark, hikers are rewarded with gorgeous mountain vistas from the trail.

Your time on the Appalachian Trail ends at the 2.7-mile mark, at which point you'll turn left to connect with a blue-blazed spur trail that takes you to Spy Rock. In a few steps, a large wooden trail kiosk educates on what to know about rare plants and camping at Spy Rock. The short version: no camping on top of Spy Rock. However, camping is allowed near the trail sign.

Over the next 0.2 mile, plan to climb steps then artfully scramble to the top of the granite dome for panoramic views across the Blue Ridge Mountains. Fall is a spectacular time to hike Spy Rock, when vibrant foliage lights up the landscape with hues of fiery orange, crimson, and amber. Stay within the fenced-in area atop Spy Rock in order to protect sensitive vegetation, including Greenland stitchwort and three-leaved cinquefoil. Even with the low fence, you will not feel restricted. You'll also be able to take lots of photos that do not include the fence. There is plenty of space on top of Spy Rock for everyone to sit and revel in the vistas. From here, retrace your steps to your vehicle. Your hike is complete.

MILES AND DIRECTIONS

0.0 Begin on a connector trail at the metal gate with "Foot Travel Welcome" sign.

0.5 Arrive at a trail sign. Turn right for the Appalachian Trail.

2.7 Turn left to pick up a blue-blazed spur trail.

From Spy Rock, take in panoramic views in all directions. In fall, the landscape is especially spectacular thanks to vibrant splashes of fiery orange and golden yellow.

2.9 Arrive at Spy Rock. Retrace your steps to the start of the trail.

5.8 Arrive back at the trailhead. Your hike is complete.

OPTION

For a longer out-and-back hike of 13 miles, start your hike from the Crabtree Falls Day Use Area on VA 56 (Crabtree Falls Highway). Hike to the top of Crabtree Falls, then continue past the falls on a trail that runs alongside Crabtree Creek. You will arrive at the Crabtree Meadows parking area at the 3.0-mile mark. From here, walk west along Meadows Lane to the start of the Spy Rock hike. Hike up to Spy Rock, then retrace your steps all the way back to the Crabtree Falls Day Use Area.

◀ Top: A hike along a southbound stretch of the white-blazed Appalachian Trail leads to 360-degree views from atop Spy Rock.

Bottom: From the granite summit, stay within the fenced-in area to protect sensitive vegetation, including Greenland stitchwort and three-leaved cinquefoil, which grows only at high elevations.

18 STONY MAN MOUNTAIN

This hike to the top of Stony Man offers a two-for-one deal on sweeping views that will leave hikers of all ages awestruck, but note that this is one of only a handful of hikes at Shenandoah National Park that is not dog-friendly.

Start: Parking area at Little Stony Man trailhead
Elevation gain: 833 feet
Distance: 3.1-mile lollipop
Difficulty: Moderate
Hiking time: 1.5 to 2 hours
Best season: Year-round
Fees and permits: $$$$
Trail contact: Shenandoah National Park, 3655 Hwy. 211 E., Luray; (540) 999-3500; www.nps.gov/shen/
Dogs: No (dogs not allowed at Stony Man Summit)

Trail surface: Mostly rock and dirt trails
Land status: National park
Nearest town: Sperryville (east) or Luray (west)
Maps: National Geographic Trails Illustrated Topographic Map 228 (Shenandoah National Park); Map 10: AT in Shenandoah National Park (Central District), PATC, Inc.
Amenities: None
Maximum grade: 30%
Cell service: Spotty

FINDING THE TRAILHEAD

The hike begins from the back of the small parking area (only eight parking spots) at the Little Stony Man trailhead on the west side of Skyline Drive at milepost 39.1. **GPS:** N38°36'20.6" / W78°21'59.7"

THE CLIMB

It's easy to find big views all across Shenandoah National Park, but it's hard to beat the two-for-one deal on this lollipop hike that includes both Stony Man (elevation 4,003 feet) and Little Stony Man Cliffs. The valley views may be the very best in the national park. Children and adults will also love splashing in the rainwater puddles at Little Stony Man Cliffs.

Arrive early to get a space in the small trailhead parking lot. The blue-blazed spur trail is adjacent to the trail sign and guides hikers up a modest hill.

In less than 0.1 mile, turn left onto the white-blazed Appalachian Trail. Over the next 0.5 mile, you'll climb 190 feet to reach Little Stony Man Cliffs at the 0.6-mile mark. Get ready to be awestruck by the tantalizing views. The rocky outcrops are plentiful, so take a seat and savor the panoramas. There are

◀ In spring and summer, yellow wildflowers adorn both sides of the Appalachian Trail between Little Stony Man Cliffs and Stony Man Mountain.

If you plan on this hike, leave the pup at home. Dogs are not allowed at the summit of Stony Man Mountain.

From the rocky overlook at Stony Man, revel in the views across the Allegheny Mountains and the Shenandoah Valley.

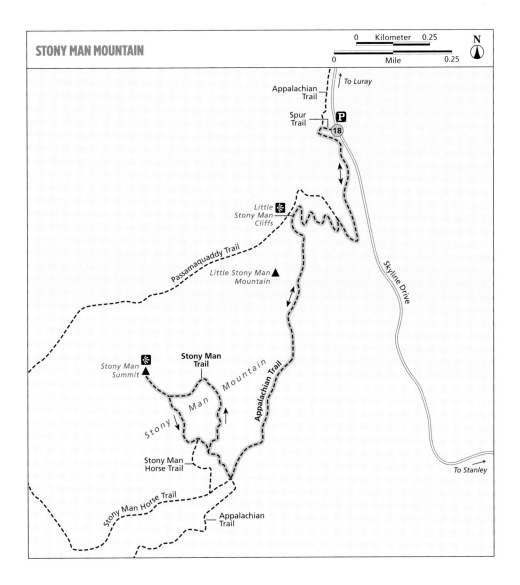

also several shallow pools that often fill up with rainwater. Continue past the cliffs along the trail into the dense forest. In spring and summer, you will be welcomed by yellow wildflowers in bloom that decorate both sides of this section of trail.

At the 1.2-mile mark, you will reach a concrete trail marker and a four-way intersection. Turn right onto the blue-blazed Stony Man Trail to navigate up the moderate incline. At the 1.5-mile mark, you will reach a navigational sign for Stony Man Summit, the second-tallest peak at Shenandoah National Park. From this point onward, dogs are strictly forbidden (as are horses).

You're now steps from the rocky outcropping that boasts breathtaking vistas of the Allegheny Mountains and Shenandoah Valley from atop Stony Man Mountain. The rocks are not hard to navigate, but you'll want to pay attention. Watch your step and stay fleet of feet as you jockey for the best views. This is one reason dogs are barred from the summit.

Take a break to splash or wade in shallow, rainwater-fed pools when you reach Little Stony Man Cliffs.

Retrace your steps from the summit, then stay left at the 1.7-mile mark to continue and complete the loop along the Stony Man Trail. You'll again come to the four-way intersection at the 1.9-mile mark. This time, turn left for the Appalachian Trail and retrace your steps to the parking area. Keep your eyes open as you walk the trail. You may see a gentle fawn nestled in tall grass or a scampering baby black bear as you hike this scenic trail.

MILES AND DIRECTIONS

0.0   Begin at the parking area at the Little Stony Man trailhead at milepost 39.1.

0.1   Turn left onto the white-blazed Appalachian Trail.

0.6   Arrive at Little Stony Man Cliffs.

1.2   Reach a four-way intersection. Turn right for Stony Man Trail.

1.5   Turn right to proceed to Stony Man Summit.

1.6   Arrive at Stony Man Summit. Retrace your steps to Stony Man Trail.

1.7   Turn left onto Stony Man Trail to complete and close the trail loop.

1.9   Reach the four-way intersection again. Turn left onto the Appalachian Trail. From here, retrace your steps to the parking area.

3.1   Arrive back at the parking area. Your hike is complete.

19 TERRAPIN MOUNTAIN

This summit hike in Bedford County wows with big views, of course, but also a watering hole, creek crossings, and colorful rhododendron thickets aplenty in the spring.

Start: Parking area on Terrapin Mountain Lane
Elevation gain: 2,638 feet
Distance: 10.3-mile lollipop
Difficulty: Strenuous
Hiking time: 5.5 to 6.5 hours
Best season: Year-round
Fees and permits: Free
Trail contact: George Washington and Jefferson National Forest (Glenwood-Pedlar Ranger District), 27 Ranger Ln., Natural Bridge

Station; (540) 291-2188; www.fs.usda.gov/detail/gwj
Dogs: Yes
Trail surface: Mostly dirt and rock trails
Land status: National forest
Nearest town: Bedford
Maps: National Geographic Trails Illustrated Topographic Map 789 (Lexington, Blue Ridge Mountains)
Amenities: None
Maximum Grade: 29%
Cell service: Fairly reliable

FINDING THE TRAILHEAD

 The trailhead is located at the back of the small gravel parking lot nearly 1 mile down Terrapin Mountain Lane. There's room for a half-dozen cars to park. When you see the "End State Maintenance" sign, you'll know you're in the right place. **GPS:** N37°31'51.1" / W79°25'42.8"

THE CLIMB

The Terrapin Mountain hike in Big Island is long and strenuous, but it's also wildly rewarding thanks to several big overlooks, cascading falls, a watering hole, and an abundance of bright pink rhododendrons that greet and encourage you along the trail in the spring. There's also a shower-like waterfall for a refreshing cool-down late in the hike.

To begin this leafy hike in the Jefferson National Forest, walk around a gate prohibiting vehicles to a rocky connector trail that guides you to the yellow-blazed Terrapin Mountain Trail. Pause at the trail kiosk to snap a photo of the trail map.

At the 0.3-mile mark, you'll see a trail sign. This is a loop trail, but your best bet is to walk straight ahead for a counterclockwise loop. Follow the sign directions for the summit. Get ready to dig deep; the trail

Snap a photo of the map for the Terrapin Mountain Trail at the trail kiosk. It's always good to have a map at the ready, just in case.

In the spring, bright pink rhododendrons line the hiking trail and encourage you as you climb to the overlooks on Terrapin Mountain.

is about to get very steep—and it's easier to tackle this grade going up than going down. In spring, rhododendrons are in bloom. It's almost as if they're cheering you up the hiking trail. While this hike is steep, it also offers many rewards, the first of which turns up at the 1.4-mile mark—a rocky outcrop with 180-degree views. Settle in, take a breather.

A second overlook is not far up the trail, but you need to be alert for this one. At the 1.8-mile mark, there is a yellow arrow spray-painted on the ground, on the left side of the trail. Follow this narrow trail 0.1 mile east to reach a rocky east-facing overlook with plentiful valley views. From here, retrace your steps, then turn left to continue climbing the Terrapin Mountain Trail. At the 2.6-mile mark, a yellow arrow painted on a tree urges you to step off the trail to savor north-facing views from a delightful rocky outcrop. Such an abundance of views, and you've not yet reached the summit of Terrapin Mountain (elevation 3,488 feet). You'll reach another trail sign at the 2.7-mile mark, for a side trail to the summit. Stay left and follow the yellow blazes—as well as one more yellow arrow—to the summit, which comes into view at the 3.0-mile mark. The south-facing views are outstanding, including Sharp Top and Flat Top. Take your time to savor the views; you've earned this time with the scenic mountain panoramas.

Once you've soaked up every last vista, retrace your steps, then stay left to reconnect with the Terrapin Mountain Trail, which you'll be back on at the 3.2-mile mark. Get ready to exit the forest—briefly—when you reach a clearing at the 3.7-mile mark. You'll see a gravel road in front of you, and you may pause in confusion. There is no signage.

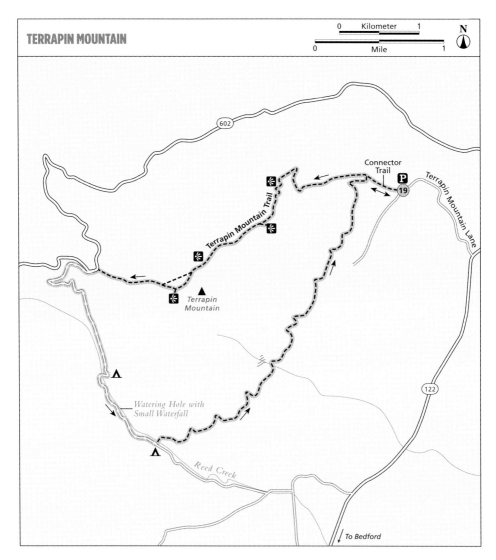

At the gravel road, turn left, but stay alert for a trail sign on the left to lead you back into the woods and on to Reed Creek.

As you descend and loop back around to the parking area, you'll come upon the flowing cascades of Reed Creek at the 5.4-mile mark. It's savagely calming. In a few more steps, there is a large primitive campsite with a supersize fire ring. Hopscotch across Reed Creek, then continue south. At the 5.8-mile mark, a path leads off on the left, to a small waterfall and a refreshing watering hole. You may want to bring water shoes since this is a great spot to wade in the creek and cool off at the waterfall. Retrace your steps, then turn left to continue south on the Terrapin Mountain Trail. Stay alert because the trail unexpectedly bears left at the 6.3-mark. You'll see another large fire ring and you'll need to cross back over Reed Creek.

From this point on, it's pretty much a simple walk in the forest, but there is one last surprise. At the 7.8-mile mark, a faint spur trail on the left leads to a shower-like waterfall.

You can stand under this waterfall and get completely soaked on a warm day. You'll close the loop of the hike at the 10.0-mile mark. Turn right onto the connector trail and return to the parking area at the 10.3-mile mark.

MILES AND DIRECTIONS

0.0 Begin at an iron gate restricting motor vehicles at the back of the parking area.

0.3 Stay straight for the yellow-blazed Terrapin Mountain Trail.

1.4 Arrive at the first rocky outcrop for mountain views.

1.8 Reach a spur trail. Turn left to a rocky overlook for east-facing views. Retrace your steps.

2.0 Turn left to continue on the Terrapin Mountain Trail.

2.6 A yellow arrow directs you to a third rocky outcrop, on the right side of the trail.

2.7 Arrive at a trail sign. Turn left for the path to the summit.

3.0 Reach the rocky summit of Terrapin Mountain for south-facing vistas. Retrace your steps, then stay left to reconnect with the Terrapin Mountain Trail.

3.2 Turn left for the Terrapin Mountain Trail.

3.7 Arrive at an open clearing. Turn left on the gravel road, then turn left at the trail sign to pick up the trail again and descend into the forest.

5.4 Reach a campsite. Cross over Reed Creek.

5.8 Turn left onto a path that leads to a small waterfall and a watering hole. Retrace your steps.

6.3 Turn left, then cross back over Reed Creek.

7.8 Turn left onto a faint spur trail that leads to a waterfall. Retrace your steps.

10.0 Close the loop, then turn right onto the connector trail to the parking area.

10.3 Arrive back at the parking area. Your hike is complete.

Top: At the 3.0-mile mark, get ready to be rewarded with south-facing views, ▶ including the peaks of Sharp Top and Flat Top.

Bottom: Bring water shoes to wade into the refreshingly cool watering hole and splash in the small waterfall that's just steps off the Terrapin Mountain Trail.

20 THREE RIDGES

Tackle this hike in one day, or break it up into two days. It's one of the most popular two-day backpacking trips in the state, boasting several vistas, waterfalls, and two hiking shelters.

Start: Reids Gap parking area
Elevation gain: 3,940 feet
Distance: 15.0-mile lollipop
Difficulty: Strenuous
Hiking time: 10 to 11 hours
Best season: Year-round
Fees and permits: Free
Trail contact: George Washington and Jefferson National Forest (Glenwood-Pedlar Ranger District), 27 Ranger Ln., Natural Bridge Station; (540) 291-2188; www.fs.usda .gov/detail/gwj

Dogs: Yes
Trail surface: Mostly dirt and rock trails
Land status: National forest
Nearest town: Tyro
Maps: National Geographic Trails Illustrated Topographic Map 791 (Staunton, Shenandoah Mountain)
Amenities: Privies at hikers' shelters
Maximum grade: 28%
Cell service: Spotty, especially at Harpers Creek Shelter

FINDING THE TRAILHEAD

 The trailhead is located at the front of the parking area at Reids Gap, which is where the Blue Ridge Parkway and VA 664 come together. There is room for fifteen to twenty cars, but the lot fills early and quickly, especially on fair-weather weekends. The marker for the Appalachian Trail is just past the last car in the parking area. **GPS:** N37°54'04.2" / W78°59'07.0"

THE CLIMB

The 15.0-mile Three Ridges lollipop hike is among the most challenging in Virginia but also among the most rewarding. The views are exceptionally scenic and are worth every bead of sweat and step you take as you complete an elevation gain of nearly 4,000 feet. Tackle this hike in one day or take two days as a backpacking trip, with an overnight at Harpers Creek Shelter. Both are fantastic ways to experience this spectacular hike, which includes a nice stretch of the Appalachian Trail.

The hike begins with a mild ascent along the white-blazed Appalachian Trail. A breezy meadow is on your right as you hike toward and into the George Washington National Forest. You'll be rewarded early on, too. At the 0.8-mile mark, you'll reach a vista that's easy to miss. Look for a primitive campsite and a fire ring on the left. Then look right. You'll see a short spur trail that leads to a rocky west-facing overlook. The views are fabulous, but they are a mere taste of what to expect from the craggy Three Ridges overlook that turns up later in the hike. Once you've soaked up the views, retrace your steps, then turn right to continue on the Appalachian Trail.

◄ Top: You will be rewarded early on this hike thanks to a west-facing vista that can be reached by way of a short spur trail at the 0.8-mile mark.
Bottom: Get ready for big mountain views at the 3.8-mile mark. Settle in on the large rocky overlook to refuel and rehydrate.

A large trail kiosk welcomes hikers at the 1.8-mile mark. Stay left here to continue on the white-blazed Appalachian Trail.

At the 1.8-mile mark, you'll arrive at an intersection and a large trail kiosk. Stay left to continue on the southbound Appalachian Trail. The real ascent to Three Ridges (elevation 3,970 feet) begins now. You'll first go up and over Bee Mountain at the 2.3-mile mark, but there are no vistas. Just keep climbing, friends. You'll reach a switchback and a set of rocky stairs at the 3.7-mile mark. Keep climbing. It's only a few more steps until you arrive at a rocky outcrop on the right with seriously booming views at the 3.8-mile mark. These are the highlight views of the hike, even though the true summit of Three Ridges is not until another mile later, at the 4.8-mile mark. There, you'll find little more than a sign indicating how much farther up the trail until the Harpers Creek Shelter, as well as a short spur trail to a campsite with a fire ring.

Once you climb up and over the actual Three Ridges summit, you'll begin to descend, then reach a few switchbacks and rock scrambles. Get ready to be wowed by another big view at the 6.2-mile mark. Pause here for the views from atop Chimney Rock. There's another wide-open view across the Blue Ridge Mountains at the 6.7-mile mark. From here, there's a switchback and one final wide-open view of the working farms in the valley at the 7.0-mile mark.

As you continue on, you'll encounter at least three rock scrambles, which are not exactly a piece of cake when wearing a backpack or daypack. At the 8.3-mile mark, you'll reach a T-junction. Stay to the right for the Harpers Creek Shelter. You'll also see a privy and a picnic table, as well as many, many campsites and fire rings that are both to the right and left. It's practically a hotel for backpackers. This is the low point of the hike elevation-wise. This is also the end of the hike if you're breaking it up into two days, so put on your camp shoes, set up your tent, and relax.

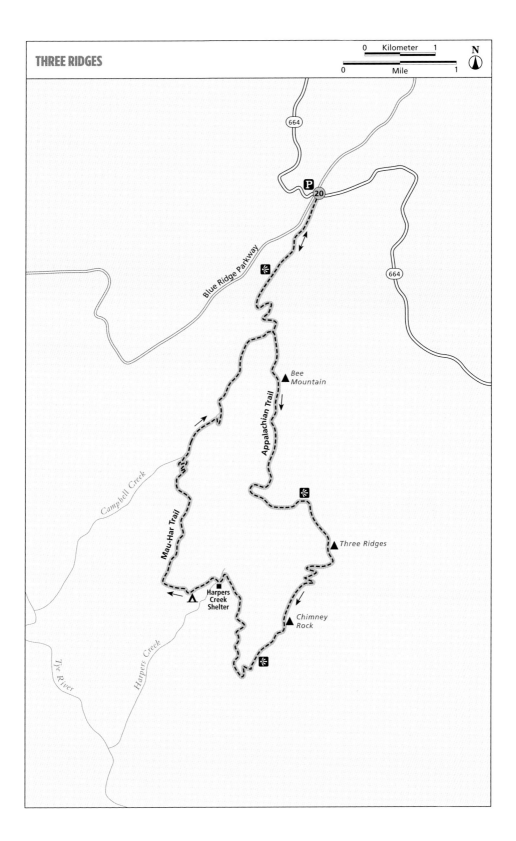

THREE RIDGES

0   Kilometer   1

0   Mile   1

N

664

P 20

Blue Ridge Parkway

Bee
Mountain

Appalachian Trail

664

Campbell Creek

Mau-Har Trail

Three Ridges

Harpers
Creek
Shelter

Chimney
Rock

Tye River

Harpers Creek

Over the course of this hike, you'll pass two hiking shelters, including the Maupin Fields Shelter at the 13.0-mile mark.

If you do this as a one-day hike, you'll need to dig deep and tap into your energy reserves as you now begin to ascend on the Appalachian Trail, first crossing over Harpers Creek. At the 9.4-mile mark, you'll reach a trail junction and a trail sign. Turn right for the blue-blazed Mau-Har Trail. You'll ascend for nearly a mile, and it's quite steep in some stretches, despite a few switchbacks. At the 11.1-mile mark, you'll reach a sign for a waterfall. A yellow-blazed spur trail leads to the waterfall, but you may see little more than a trickle in the heat of summer when water levels are low. Still, there might be a few gentle cascades.

From here, you'll hike parallel to Campbell Creek for much of the next 1.9 miles. It's nearly all uphill, too. There are a few spots to step out to splash in watering holes on the way. You'll arrive at the Maupin Fields Shelter at the 13.0-mile mark. Enjoy a snack or rehydrate at the picnic table before the final push. You'll close the loop at the 13.2-mile mark when you reach the large trail sign. Turn left to reconnect with the Appalachian Trail. You'll finish at the Reids Gap parking area at the 15.0-mile mark.

MILES AND DIRECTIONS

0.0 Begin at the trailhead for the Appalachian Trail at the front of the parking area at Reids Gap.

0.8 Arrive at a spur trail on the right that leads to a vista. Retrace your steps to the main trail, then turn right to continue on.

1.8 Reach a trail kiosk and a trail junction. Stay left for the Appalachian Trail.

3.8 Break for big views from a rocky overlook.

6.2 Pause for more big views from Chimney Rock.

8.3 Reach a T-junction. A spur trail on the right leads to the Harpers Creek Shelter. Retrace your steps to the Appalachian Trail.

9.4 Arrive at a trail junction. Turn right for the Mau-Har Trail.

11.1 Reach a sign and a waterfall on the left (best in early spring).

13.0 Arrive at the Maupin Fields Shelter.

13.2 Reach a trail junction. Stay left for the Appalachian Trail. Retrace your steps to the parking area.

15.0 Arrive back at the Reids Gap parking area. Your hike is complete.

OPTION

As an alternative to this strenuous lollipop hike, a good option is a more moderate out-and-back hike to the primary overlook. Hike 3.8 miles south on the Appalachian Trail to the overlook, then retrace your steps for a rewarding 7.6-mile hike.

SOUTHWEST VIRGINIA

Southwest Virginia is a breathtakingly rugged section of the state made up of valleys, ridges, and gaps as well as scenic rivers, grassy balds, and highlands. This less-trafficked region goes unseen by large swaths of residents and visitors in Virginia, but this glorious landscape inspires with sensational panoramas that leave many visitors, even longtime residents, especially awestruck.

Many consider the far-reaching vistas in Southwest Virginia to surpass those in the other mountainous regions. It's this slice of Virginia where you'll find Mount Rogers, the state's highpoint, which stands at 5,729 feet tall (though sadly has no views, only a survey marker). Several summit hikes are clustered together in this high-elevation section, including Mount Rogers and Buzzard Rock. At Grayson Highlands State Park, the relatively easy hike at Haw Orchard Mountain leads to two rocky overlooks, including Big Pinnacle and Little Pinnacle. The views across the highlands and alpine meadows in Grayson and Smyth Counties are hypnotic.

In Giles County, a stone's throw from Mountain Lake Lodge (the stone lodge where *Dirty Dancing* was filmed), is Sugar Run Mountain and Pearis Mountain. Both hikes snake along the Appalachian Trail, rewarding with hikers' shelters, big views, high-elevation ponds, and plentiful rhododendrons in late spring.

In this region, you'll also find hikes that are serious two-for-one deals. Not two big summits, but a summit and something else really cool, like a massive sand cave or a sandstone labyrinth. The White Rocks hike, for example, first leads to a large sand cave with an acre of beach-like sand, before reaching the White Rocks overlook late in the hike. Incredible.

Every hike in this section has been hand-picked and hiker-tested, so you're guaranteed to love every summit you climb in Southwest Virginia. Get ready to hit the trails.

◀ Sit and stay awhile as you soak in the mesmerizing views from the top of Buffalo Mountain near Floyd.

21 BUFFALO MOUNTAIN

This easy loop hike at Buffalo Mountain Natural Area Preserve affords big views from a critical natural area preserve that is home to rare plants and animals, including a species of mealybug found only in this subalpine area.

Start: Buffalo Mountain Natural Area Preserve parking area
Elevation gain: 587 feet
Distance: 2.0-mile lollipop
Difficulty: Easy
Hiking time: 1 to 1.5 hours
Best season: Year-round
Fees and permits: Free
Trail contact: Virginia Department of Conservation and Recreation, 5162 Valleypointe Parkway, Roanoke; (540) 265-5234; www.dcr.virginia .gov/natural-heritage/natural-area -preserves/buffalo

Dogs: No
Trail surface: Mostly dirt and rock trails, some rock scrambles and wooden steps
Land status: Natural area preserve
Nearest town: Floyd
Maps: Printable map at www.dcr .virginia.gov/natural-heritage /document/pgbuffalo.pdf
Amenities: Porta-potty in the parking lot
Maximum grade: 18%
Cell service: Fairly reliable

FINDING THE TRAILHEAD

The trailhead is located at the back of the small (space for ten cars) parking area for Buffalo Mountain Natural Area Preserve, located at the end of a nearly 2-mile gravel road. There is nowhere else to park, so when the lot is full, it's full—meaning you'll need to find another hike to do. **GPS:** N36°47'12.9" / W80°27'01.5"

THE CLIMB

Buffalo Mountain Natural Area Preserve in Floyd County is not only home to one of the tallest peaks in Virginia, Buffalo Mountain (3,971 feet), it's also a critical habitat that supports more than a dozen rare plants and animals on the open, grassy peak. Sensitive vegetation includes bog bluegrass, three-leaved cinquefoil, and mountain sandwort. Buffalo Mountain is also the only known habitat—in the world—of a rare mealybug called *Puto kosztarabi*. The mealybug was named in 1993 for Michael Kosztarab, the local entomologist who first observed the insect.

Given the biodiversity at the round, treeless summit of Buffalo Mountain, you'll find a rocky path at the top that's roped off to carefully guide visitors and protect sensitive vegetation from inadvertently being trampled and destroyed. Not to worry, despite the regulated path, there are plenty of rocky spots to sit and savor the 360-degree views from the top of the mountain. It's important to stay on marked trails at all times to preserve and protect the subalpine vegetation.

◄ Top: This easy hike to the top of Buffalo Mountain begins on the red-blazed Oak Trail, which affords scenic views of neighboring mountains through leafless trees in the winter months.

Bottom: As you return to the parking area, take the blue-blazed Ridge Trail, a shorter path that includes three dozen wooden steps to help ease the descent as you complete this hike.

The rounded, treeless summit of Buffalo Mountain wows with 360-degree views across Southwest Virginia from two rocky outcrops.

In the parking lot, you'll see a large trail kiosk identifying three hiking trails: Oak Trail (red), Ridge Trail (blue), and Barrens Loop (orange). It's a cinch to cobble together the three trails to construct a wooded loop with a stop for big views.

From the trail kiosk, the Oak Trail sets off to the left. On the right, you'll see wooden steps that ascend the mountain by way of the Ridge Trail. You can start in either direction, but for this hike, we'll start on the Oak Trail for a clockwise hike. Both trails end at Barrens Loop, which leads hikers along the final steps to the exposed summit of Buffalo Mountain.

Starting on the red-blazed Oak Trail, the path guides you along several forested switchbacks as you ascend more than 400 feet over 0.9 mile to the start of Barrens Loop. Turn left at the trail marker and follow the orange blazes along Barrens Loop. From here, you'll continue climbing for another 0.3 mile until you reach the roped off loop that encircles the open summit. There are two large exposed outcrops that are just right for scrambling and relaxing with a well-deserved snack. You'll want to stay for a while, as the vistas across the mountains are that intoxicating, but do mind the fragile vegetation.

Once you've taken in all the views, retrace your steps to the trail marker at the start of Barrens Loop. From here, continue straight ahead to pick up the blue-blazed Ridge Trail. This 0.5-mile trail is a more direct route to the parking lot. You'll encounter a few switchbacks on the way, but the bulk of the elevation change is by way of three dozen steps at the very end of the trail. At the 2.0-mile mark, your hike is complete.

MILES AND DIRECTIONS

0.0 Begin to the left of the trail kiosk in the parking lot. Start on the red-blazed Oak Trail.

0.9 Reach a trail junction. Turn left for the orange-blazed Barrens Loop.

1.2 Arrive at a loop path at the summit of Buffalo Mountain. Retrace your steps to the trail marker at the start of Barrens Loop.

1.5 Continue straight ahead for the blue-blazed Ridge Trail.

2.0 Arrive back at the parking area. Your hike is complete.

BUFFALO MOUNTAIN

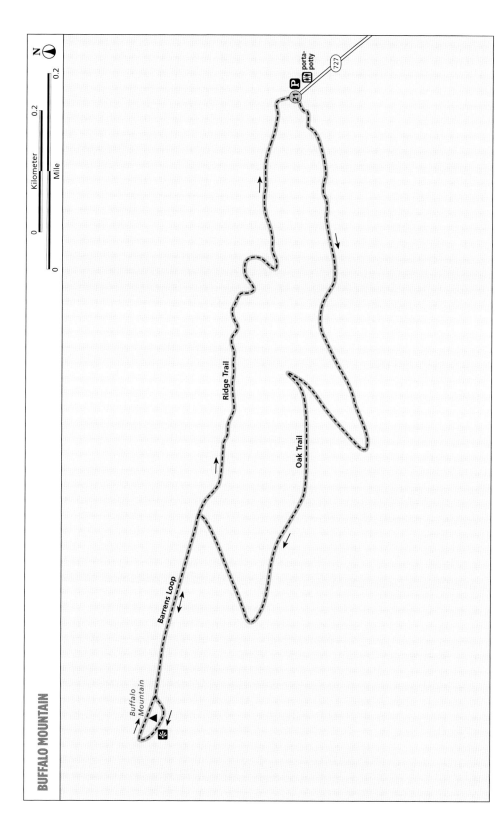

N

Kilometer
0   0.2   0.2

Mile
0   0.2

Buffalo
Mountain

Barrens Loop

Ridge Trail

Oak Trail

21 P

porta-
potty

727

22 BUZZARD ROCK

This hike inspires with far-reaching views across lush open balds and pristine mountain panoramas in all directions from Buzzard Rock near Damascus.

Start: Parking area on Beech Mountain Road
Elevation gain: 1,581 feet
Distance: 4.8 miles out and back
Difficulty: Moderate
Hiking time: 3 to 4 hours
Best season: Year-round
Fees and permits: Free
Trail contact: George Washington and Jefferson National Forest (Eastern Divide Ranger District), 110 Southpark Dr., Blacksburg; (540) 552-4641; www.fs.usda.gov/detail /gwj

Dogs: Yes
Trail surface: Mostly dirt and rock trails
Land status: National forest
Nearest town: Damascus
Maps: National Geographic Trails Illustrated Topographic Map 1503 (Appalachian Trail: Damascus to Bailey Gap)
Amenities: None
Maximum grade: 28%
Cell service: Unreliable, especially at the trailhead

FINDING THE TRAILHEAD

The trailhead is located at the back of the small parking area on Beech Mountain Road. **GPS:** N36°38'13.9" / W81°38'25.9"

THE CLIMB

There is more than one Buzzard Rock hike in Virginia, but this hike along the Appalachian Trail to lush grassy balds near Damascus is one to love. It's even worthy of a spot on your hiking bucket list. The views are incomparable, and you may even feel like you're on top of the world, especially after climbing more than one hundred steps to the top. You may feel more like you're climbing a stairway to heaven.

You will see an Appalachian Trail sign on the opposite side of the road, but this hike is along a northbound stretch and begins on the same side of the road as the lot. It's also worth noting (AT&T users, pay attention) that there is no cell signal in the parking lot, but you will get a bar or two on the way to Buzzard Rock. At the back of the lot, you will see a trail lead off into the dense forest. Start here for the gradual ascent to Buzzard Rock.

At the 0.4-mile mark, you'll reach a spring spigot for drinking water. Refill your bottle, if you like, but know that it's always a good idea to purify all water with a portable water filtration system before drinking. As you continue on, you'll approach a switchback and a half-dozen or so wooden steps built into the trail at the 0.5-mile mark. Then you'll negotiate more steps, another switchback, more steps, and finally, a clearing at the

◀ Top: The open balds at Buzzard Rock are especially lush and green in spring and summer.

Bottom: The author stands at the false summit, taking in the views in all directions across Southwest Virginia.

There are at least one hundred stone steps that lead up to Buzzard Rock, which make you feel like you are ascending to heaven.

2.2-mile mark. After more than 2.0 miles ascending in the dense, shaded woods, you will again see the sun. Slather on the sunblock.

From here, the climb continues on stone steps built into the trail. Dig deep to climb seventy-nine steps to reach a rocky overlook at the 2.3-mile mark. This small viewpoint is a false summit—Buzzard Rock is still just ahead—but the wide-open vistas will bowl you over. It's another twenty-one or so steps up to a grassy bald and Buzzard Rock, which comes into view at the 2.4-mile mark. Buzzard Rock is much larger than the first rocky overlook and is good for a scramble to the top for views across to Beech Mountain.

At this point, you are just below Whitetop Mountain, the second-tallest mountain in Virginia. You can continue on up, but there is nothing to see beyond a building with satellite towers and a heavily restricted and fenced-off area. Surely, more than a few people must venture up to reach the second-highest point in the state. You may, however, want to follow the tire tracks up to the gravel road for Whitetop. To do so, stay left of the Appalachian Trail as you continue past Buzzard Rock. The views across the grassy bald and Buzzard Rock from a higher elevation are exceptional. This side adventure would add another mile or two onto this hike. Assuming a turnaround at Buzzard Rock, this hike clocks in at 4.8 miles round-trip.

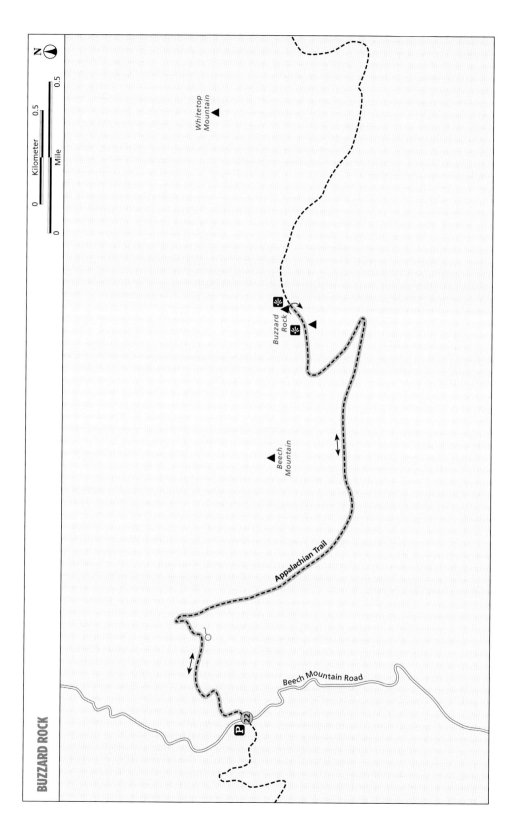

BUZZARD ROCK

Scramble to the top of Buzzard Rock to savor far-reaching views across to Beech Mountain.

MILES AND DIRECTIONS

0.0 Begin from the back of the parking area on Beech Mountain Road. (Note that the trailhead is on the same side of the road as the parking lot.)

0.4 Reach a freshwater spring on the left side of the trail.

2.2 Arrive at an open clearing as the forest opens up.

2.3 Reach the false summit.

2.4 Arrive at Buzzard Rock. Retrace your steps to the parking area.

4.8 Arrive back at the parking lot. Your hike is complete.

23 CHESTNUT KNOB

This summit hike wows with a stone hikers' shelter, as well as panoramas across Burke's Garden, a bucolic bowl-shaped valley entirely encircled by Garden Mountain.

Start: Parking area on Medley Valley Road
Elevation gain: 778 feet
Distance: 2.8 miles out and back
Difficulty: Moderate
Hiking time: 1.5 to 2 hours
Best season: Year-round
Fees and permits: Free
Trail contact: George Washington and Jefferson National Forest (Eastern Divide Ranger District), 110 Southpark Dr., Blacksburg; (540) 552-4641; www.fs.usda.gov/detail/gwj
Dogs: Yes
Trail surface: Mostly dirt and rock trails
Land status: National forest
Nearest town: Tazewell
Maps: National Geographic Trails Illustrated Topographic Map 1503 (Appalachian Trail: Damascus to Bailey Gap)
Amenities: None
Maximum grade: 25%
Cell service: Reliable
Special considerations: The gravel road leading to the parking area is bumpy and not well-suited for sedans. A four-wheel-drive vehicle is recommended.

FINDING THE TRAILHEAD

The trailhead is located on the north side of the small parking area (space for three or four cars) on Medley Valley Road, 0.4 mile past the "End State Maintenance" sign. Just beyond the parking lot is a primitive campsite with a fire ring and three log stumps that serve as chairs or small tables. **GPS:** N37°03'19.3" / W81°22'49.7"

THE CLIMB

The hike to the top of Chestnut Knob (elevation 4,409 feet) is worthwhile as much for the hikers' shelter that sits at the summit as for the sweeping panoramas across Burke's Garden. It's a short hike, too, less than 3.0 miles with a manageable ascent. Your biggest challenge of the day may be reaching the trailhead. The last 0.4 mile along a pothole-laden gravel road is a doozy. It's definitely not for everyone, and it's certainly not suitable for all vehicles.

The hike begins with a handful of steps. Interestingly, despite a start on the north, you will hike along a southbound section of the Appalachian Trail. The forested climb begins immediately, but the grade frequently fluctuates. It's definitely not one long, steep trek to the top. There are a few switchbacks, too. There's not much to see on the way up, but it's a short hike with sizable rewards for not a lot of effort.

The forest opens up to a clearing at the 1.3-mile mark. You'll see the stone hikers' shelter straight ahead. This shelter is one of sixty-two hikers' shelters along the Appalachian Trail in Virginia. It's unique too in that it's got four stone walls and a door (most are three-sided wooden shelters). This shelter with eight bunks and a table inside was once an old fire warden's cabin. Just beyond the shelter are a privy and a sign noting that you

Hike along a southbound stretch of the white-blazed Appalachian Trail in Burke's Garden to reach the top of Chestnut Knob.

◀ Top: The Chestnut Knob Shelter is one of sixty-two hikers' shelters along the Appalachian Trail in Virginia.
Bottom: Inside the Chestnut Knob Shelter, you'll find eight bunks and a wooden table.

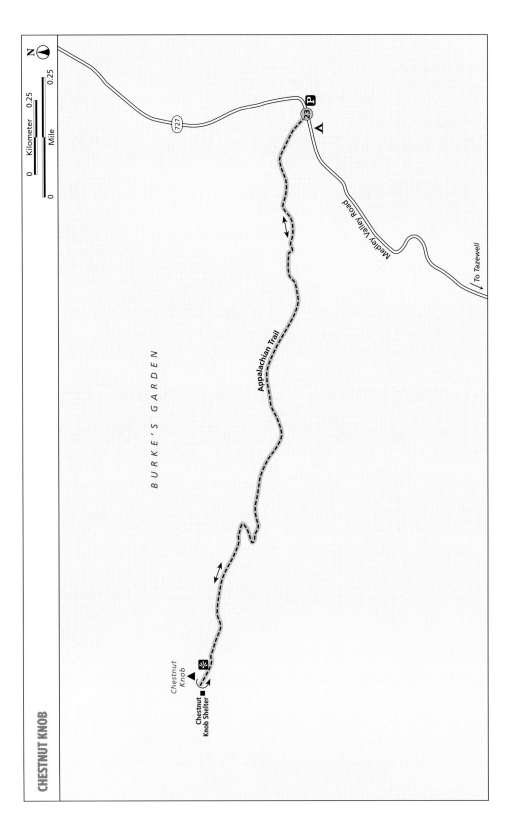

CHESTNUT KNOB

N

0   Kilometer   0.25

0   Mile   0.25

727

Medley Valley Road

To Tazewell

P
23

Appalachian Trail

BURKE'S GARDEN

Chestnut Knob

Chestnut
Knob Shelter

are in Beartown Wilderness, a 5,609-acre swath of remote wilderness within the Jefferson National Forest in eastern Tazewell County.

To the northeast of the shelter is a wide-open view of Burke's Garden, which is completely encircled by Garden Mountain. This bucolic, bowl-shaped farming valley is the highest valley in Virginia, and is even referred to as "God's Thumbprint." This fertile valley was discovered by surveyor James Burke in 1750, who, according to lore, buried potato peelings in the valley. A later group exploring the valley discovered the potatoes, but as a full-grown crop. The panoramas are especially spectacular at sunrise, if you can make the climb early in the morning.

Note that the grass in this clearing can be tall and unruly, so it's a good idea to wear long pants on this hike, especially in spring and summer. Once you've taken in all the views, retrace your steps to the trailhead to complete the hike at the 2.8-mile mark.

MILES AND DIRECTIONS

0.0 Begin on the north side of the parking area, on the southbound section of the Appalachian Trail.

1.3 The forest opens up to a clearing, and you will see Chestnut Knob Shelter ahead.

1.4 Arrive at Chestnut Knob Shelter, as well as a Burke's Garden overlook. Retrace your steps to the parking area.

2.8 Arrive back at the parking area. Your hike is complete.

From the Raccoon Branch Campground in Sugar Grove, hike to the site of a former fire tower atop Dickey Knob. Along the way, pause for an overlook with breathtaking views across the Rye Valley.

Start: Raccoon Branch Campground	**Dogs:** Yes
Elevation gain: 932 feet	**Trail surface:** Mostly dirt and rock trails
Distance: 4.8 miles out and back	
Difficulty: Moderate	**Land status:** National forest
Hiking time: 2 to 3 hours	**Nearest town:** Marion
Best season: Year-round	**Maps:** National Geographic Trails
Fees and permits: $	Illustrated Topographic Map 1503
Trail contact: George Washington	(Appalachian Trail: Damascus to
and Jefferson National Forest	Bailey Gap)
(Mount Rogers National Recreation	**Amenities:** Restrooms and picnic
Area), 3714 Hwy. 16, Marion; (276)	tables at the campground
783-5196; www.fs.usda.gov/detail	**Maximum grade:** 14%
/gwj	**Cell service:** None

FINDING THE TRAILHEAD

The trailhead is located at a wooden footbridge on the west side of the Raccoon Branch Campground. **GPS:** N36°44'46.6" / W81°25'30.0"

THE CLIMB

A forested hike on the Dickey Knob Trail leads to the top of Dickey Knob (elevation 3,606 feet), which was at one time the site of a fire tower overlooking Atkins and Damascus. Built in 1934, the fire tower stood watch for sixty years before it was removed in 1994. Today, all that remains is five concrete foundation blocks. The area became a part of the Raccoon Branch Wilderness, which is accessed by way of the Raccoon Branch Campground near Sugar Grove.

On arrival at Raccoon Branch Campground, you'll notice that there are no parking spaces, at least not for day visitors. All the sites appear to be set aside for overnight campers. The scoop—from the mouth of the on-duty campground host—is that it's okay to park in any space not marked as reserved. The trailhead is located on the west side of the campground, so the first sites you see as you drive in on a one-way counterclockwise loop are your best bets.

Look for the wooden bridge that crosses over Dickey Creek. Once across, you'll reach a sign for Raccoon Branch Wilderness. Turn right here to continue on the unmarked trail to Dickey Knob. In a few more steps, you can step out to the creek for a refreshing splash at this popular trout stream either before or after your hike. At the 0.1-mile mark, you'll pass a bench, then cross a wooden bridge, then pass a second bench. The trail then forks at the 0.2-mile mark. Stay right to ascend the trail to Dickey Knob.

◀ Your first steps on this trail guide you across a wooden bridge over gently flowing Dickey Creek.

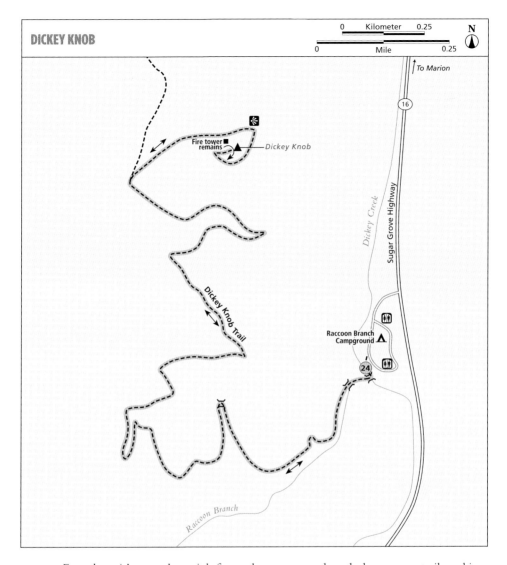

From here, it's a mostly straightforward ascent, even though there are no trail markings of any kind. Cross over a third footbridge at the 0.5-mile mark, then get ready to zigzag up the trail by way of a few trail switchbacks. There's the potential for confusion at the 2.0-mile mark when you see two separate trails that go uphill. Follow the trail with the sign featuring a hiker icon. Continue on and you'll reach a beautiful overlook with scenic vistas across the Rye Valley and Sugar Grove at the 2.3-mile mark. You'll definitely want to snap and share this view on Instagram.

Make a right turn at the 2.4-mile mark. You're now only a few steps from Dickey Knob. Take time to check out the fire tower ruins, as well as the survey marker that

◀ Top: At the 2.0-mile mark, you will see two trails that seem to ascend to Dickey Knob. The trail with the hiker sign is the route to choose.

Bottom: An overlook at the 2.4-mile mark rewards with big views across Sugar Grove and the Rye Valley.

At the summit, keep your eyes open for the survey marker that was placed in 1934 to mark the top of Dickey Knob.

was placed in 1934 to mark the top of Dickey Knob. Once you've explored the forested area (there are no views from the knob), retrace your steps to the trailhead. Your hike is complete at the 4.8-mile mark.

MILES AND DIRECTIONS

0.0 Begin at a wooden footbridge over Dickey Creek on the west side of Raccoon Branch Campground. Once across the bridge, turn right.

0.2 At the fork, stay right for the Dickey Knob Trail.

2.0 At the fork, take the trail with the hiker icon sign to reach Dickey Knob.

2.3 Arrive at an overlook on the left with views across the Rye Valley and Sugar Grove.

2.4 Reach the top of Dickey Knob. Retrace your steps to the trailhead.

4.8 Arrive back at the trailhead. Your hike is complete.

This short and sweet hike at Grayson Highlands State Park guides visitors to far-reaching vistas from atop two of Virginia's highest peaks: Big Pinnacle and Little Pinnacle.

Start: Massie Gap parking area
Elevation gain: 547 feet
Distance: 2.1-mile lollipop
Difficulty: Moderate
Hiking time: 1.5 to 2 hours
Best season: Year-round
Fees and permits: $$
Trail contact: Grayson Highlands State Park, 829 Grayson Highland Ln., Mouth of Wilson; (276) 579-7092; www.dcr.virginia.gov/state-parks/grayson-highlands
Dogs: Yes

Trail surface: Mostly dirt and gravel trails, some rock scrambles
Land status: State park
Nearest town: Marion
Maps: National Geographic Trails Illustrated Topographic Map 786 (Mount Rogers National Recreation Area)
Amenities: Restrooms at visitor center
Maximum grade: 14%
Cell service: Spotty

FINDING THE TRAILHEAD

The Big Pinnacle Trail begins on the south side of the Massie Gap parking area on Grayson Highland Lane. **GPS:** N36°38'00.1" / W81°30'31.5"

THE CLIMB

Grayson Highlands State Park in Southwest Virginia is best known for its free-roaming wild ponies that can frequently be seen along a section of the white-blazed Appalachian Trail that cuts across the top of this park. However, Grayson Highlands is also where to go to hike to several of the state's highest peaks, including Big Pinnacle and Little Pinnacle. Technically, Big Pinnacle is the peak of Haw Orchard Mountain (elevation 5,068 feet). It's also less than 0.5 mile from Little Pinnacle (5,089 feet). Both can be reached by way of the yellow-blazed Big Pinnacle Trail and the red-blazed Twin Pinnacles Trail.

When you arrive at the parking area, you may see that most parking spaces are occupied, but not to worry, the vast majority of visitors are setting off to the north of the lot, to Wilburn Ridge in search of wild ponies. The start of the Big Pinnacle Trail is on the south side of the lot, and despite big views, this trail is far less trafficked by park-goers.

The hike to Big Pinnacle is short and wooded, but also flanked by wildflowers, like mountain laurel and rosebay rhododendron. In just 0.3 mile you'll reach a rocky spur trail on the right that leads to the top of Big Pinnacle. You'll need to climb steps and tap into your rock scrambling skills, but you'll be blown away by the views. Maybe literally; the winds can be rather strong. Just look at the twisted red spruce trees, which no doubt have been impacted by wind gusts.

Settle in for a snack with a side of 360-degree panoramas. You won't want to leave this peak, ever. When you do decide to move on, retrace your steps along the spur trail. Turn right at the 0.4-mile mark toward the Twin Pinnacles Trail. You'll reach a fork at the 0.5-mile mark. Both paths are the Twin Pinnacles Trail, but stay right for a direct route to

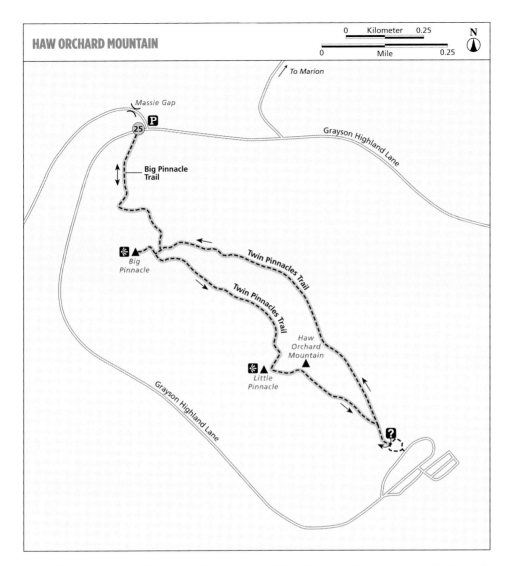

Little Pinnacle, which you will reach at the 0.9-mile mark. Interestingly, Little Pinnacle is 21 feet taller than Big Pinnacle.

There's a small rocky outcrop at Little Pinnacle, but no rock scramble is required. If you're unsure about scrambling Big Pinnacle, you'll find plenty of awe-inspiring views from Little Pinnacle, though the mountain vistas are not 360-degree views. Instead, they afford near 270-degree views. Continue on and you will arrive at a fork in the trail at the 1.2-mile mark. Stay right for the visitor center. Spend some time chatting up rangers and exploring exhibits on pioneer life, as well as local plant and animal life, then backtrack less than 0.1 mile to the fork on the Twin Pinnacles Trail. Stay to the right for a more

◀ Top: After ogling the views from Big Pinnacle and Twin Pinnacle, enjoy a wooded hike to close the loop and return to the parking area by way of the yellow-blazed Big Pinnacle Trail.
Bottom: A short spur trail to Big Pinnacle involves rocky steps and moderate rock scrambles to reach the top of one of Virginia's highest peaks.

forested hike on the return to the parking area. At the 1.7-mile mark you will reach the spur trail to Big Pinnacle. Stay right to connect with the Big Pinnacle Trail. Your hike is complete at the 2.1-mile mark.

MILES AND DIRECTIONS

0.0 Start at the trailhead for the Big Pinnacle Trail on the south side of the Massie Gap parking area.

0.3 Turn right to scramble up a short spur trail to reach Big Pinnacle. Retrace your steps.

0.4 Turn right for the Twin Pinnacles Trail.

0.5 Stay right for the Twin Pinnacles Trail.

0.9 Arrive at Little Pinnacle.

1.2 Arrive at a fork, then stay right for the visitor center. Retrace your steps to the fork.

1.3 Stay right for the Twin Pinnacles Trail.

1.7 Arrive at the spur trail to Big Pinnacle. Stay right for the Big Pinnacle Trail.

2.1 Arrive back at the trailhead and parking area. Your hike is complete.

OPTION

Alternatively, you can begin this hike at the visitor center. Stay left at the fork for the Twin Pinnacles Trail to reach Little Pinnacle and Big Pinnacle. Return by way of the forested left-most Twin Pinnacles Trail to create a 1.8-mile loop. Note that this alternative can only be completed in-season when the visitor center is open because Grayson Highland Lane is closed just past the Massie Gap parking area from mid-October to mid-May.

Top: Get ready to savor big 360-degree views from the rocky top of Big Pinnacle. ▶
Bottom: You don't need to work hard to savor the views from atop Little Pinnacle, which is just steps off the Twin Pinnacles Trail. No rock scramble required.

26 HIGH ROCKS

Navigate a rocky trail to the top of High Rocks for north-facing views across all of Wytheville, including the unofficial town emblem, a rainbow-colored water tower.

Start: Big Survey Wildlife Management Area parking area
Elevation gain: 600 feet
Distance: 2.9 miles out and back
Difficulty: Moderate
Hiking time: 1.5 to 2 hours
Best season: Year-round
Fees and permits: $
Trail contact: Virginia Department of Wildlife Resources, PO Box 90778, Henrico; (804) 367-1000; https://dwr.virginia.gov
Dogs: Yes

Trail surface: Mostly dirt and rock trails, creek crossings, some gravel trails
Land status: Wildlife management area
Nearest town: Wytheville
Maps: National Geographic Trails Illustrated Topographic Map 773 (New River Blueway)
Amenities: None
Maximum grade: 21%
Cell service: Reliable

FINDING THE TRAILHEAD

The trailhead is located at the back of the first parking area at the Big Survey Wildlife Management Area. Two adjacent lots are able to accommodate at least a couple dozen cars. **GPS:** N36°54'22.9" / W81°02'33.6"

THE CLIMB

There are two ways to the top of High Rocks (elevation 3,645 feet) in Wytheville. The path you choose depends on how much gas you have in the tank, as one route is nearly 7 miles longer than the other. Both lead to spectacular views north across all of Wytheville, including to the town's rainbow-colored water tower that pays homage to the Wytheville Chautauqua Festival and Balloon Rally that takes place every June.

The Big Survey Wildlife Management Area sits atop four mountain ridges in Wythe County. A four-wheel-drive vehicle helps, as the last miles to the lot are bumpy and gravelly, but it's not a necessity. Look for large rocks with orange spray paint in the upper lot that mark the trailhead. It's an easy trail to follow, but note that there are few painted blue blazes on trees to guide you to the top of High Rocks.

For the first 0.3 mile, the High Rocks Trail runs parallel to a gravel service road before the path deviates and leads hikers into the forested wildlife management area. The trail then narrows and becomes rockier. Rhododendron thickets line the trail. At some points, it feels more like you're hiking through a ravine than along a hiking trail, but the rewards will be plentiful when you reach High Rocks.

The trail flattens out at the 0.9-mile mark and soon reveals sizable rocks on the left as the trail embraces worthy hikers with abundant shade. At the 1.3-mile mark, your final ascent begins. In another 0.1 mile, you will reach the small but scenic overlook. A bench at the top welcomes and encourages hikers to settle in for the views. As space is limited at the top, it's wise to get an early start or to hike at an off-peak time, such as midweek, to enjoy the serenity of High Rocks.

From High Rocks, savor spectacular north-facing views across Wytheville from a quiet, rocky outcrop.

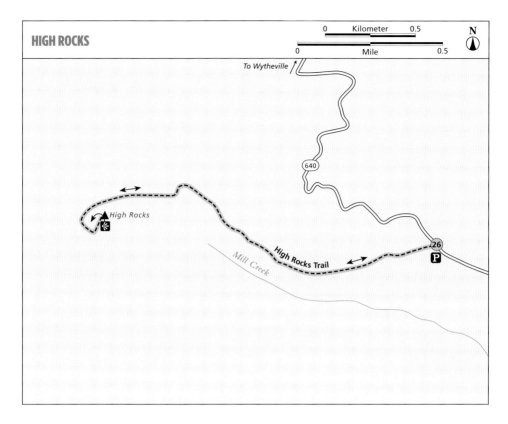

Once you've savored all the north-facing views, retrace your steps to complete this hike. The blue-blazed rock leads to your parking area. The orange-blazed rock returns hikers by way of the High Rocks Spur Trail, which is part of the longer 9.2-mile hike that originates at Crystal Springs Recreation Area.

MILES AND DIRECTIONS

0.0 Begin from the back of the parking area for the Big Survey Wildlife Management Area.

1.4 Arrive at High Rocks. Retrace your steps on the blue-blazed trail to return to your vehicle.

2.9 Arrive back at the parking area. Your hike is complete.

◀ Top: Hikers walk alongside a gravel service road for the first 0.3 mile of the hike along the High Rocks Trail.

Bottom: Much of the hike to High Rocks leads visitors through the wooded Big Survey Wildlife Management Area.

The rocky outcrop is small, but the views are big from the summit of High Rocks. Take a seat on the rocks or on the small bench that welcomes hikers.

OPTION

A longer 9.2-mile out-and-back hike to High Rocks begins at Crystal Springs Recreation Area. Start clockwise on the red-blazed Crystal Springs Loop, then turn right onto the white-blazed Boundary Trail. This trail leads to the orange-blazed High Rocks Spur Trail, which delivers hikers to High Rocks. Along the way, you'll see five backcountry campsites, as well as a small waterfall and picnic tables.

This hike wows with both big views—as far as Mount Rogers and Whitetop Mountain, two of the state's tallest peaks—and a curious sandstone maze set high atop Clinch Mountain.

Start: Parking area on VA 80
Elevation gain: 1,555 feet
Distance: 6.6 miles out and back
Difficulty: Moderate
Hiking time: 5 to 6 hours
Best season: Year-round
Fees and permits: Free
Trail contact: Virginia Department of Conservation and Recreation, 600 E. Main St., 24th Floor, Richmond; (804) 786-6124; https://dcr.virginia .gov
Dogs: Yes

Trail surface: Mostly dirt and gravel trails
Land status: State natural area preserve
Nearest town: Abingdon
Maps: National Geographic Trails Illustrated Topographic Map 786 (Mount Rogers National Recreation Area)
Amenities: None
Maximum grade: 23%
Cell service: Spotty

FINDING THE TRAILHEAD

The trailhead is located at the parking area on VA 80 for Channels Natural Area Preserve. **GPS:** N36°51'52.7" / W81°56'49.2"

THE CLIMB

Much like the hike to White Rocks in Ewing, the views are not the main attraction on the hike to Middle Knob (elevation 4,417 feet) near Abingdon, though the vistas are spectacular and well worth your time and efforts over 3.3 miles to the summit. Truth be told, the primary reason hikers climb the Brumley Mountain Trail is to reach the Great Channels of Virginia, a curious sandstone maze of slot canyon–like crevices. It's like nothing else you will see, certainly not in Virginia. Thanks to just ten parking spaces, and local authorities that are quick to tow cars for parking violations, the early bird gets the worm, as they say. In this case, it's the opportunity to check off this bucket list hike in Southwest Virginia.

This hike through Channels State Forest begins on easy gravel terrain and crosses private property for the first mile of the well-shaded trek. At the 0.2-mile mark, you'll reach a turnoff on the right for the Raven Ridge Lodge. Stay to the left and press on. Honestly, it feels like quite a slog at times, but you will soon be doubly rewarded, with big views and the natural sandstone maze. At the 0.5-mark, enjoy the power-line vista to the left of the hiking trail.

The trail splits once more at the 0.6-mile mark. Again, stay to the left to access what's more of a foot trail than a wide gravel road. Near the 1.0-mile mark, you will see a few private cabins to the right. Just past the cabins, the trail turns from mostly gravel to mostly dirt terrain. You will see a sign for The Channels. In a few more steps, a large trail kiosk appears on the right, then an iron gate that you can (legally) walk around to continue on this hike.

Keep in mind that it can be very easy to get lost in the large sandstone maze atop Clinch Mountain. Leave a backpack or water bottle at the entrance to help you find your way out.

MIDDLE KNOB

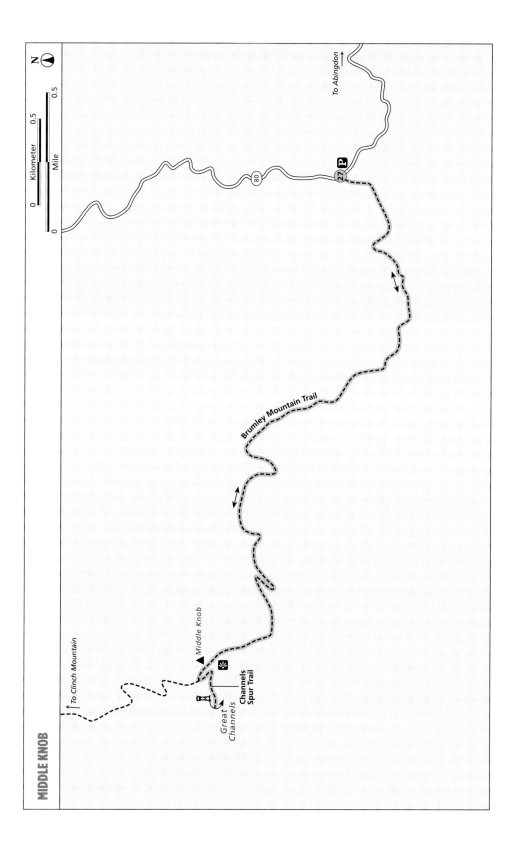

To Clinch Mountain

Great Channels

Middle Knob

Channels Spur Trail

Brumley Mountain Trail

To Abingdon

80

27 P

N

Kilometer

0   0.5

Mile

0   0.5

Once you reach the Channels Spur Trail, you're less than 0.3 mile from wide-open vistas, as well as a curious maze of slot canyon–like crevices

From the overlook, you can see as far as Mount Rogers and Whitetop Mountain, Virginia's two tallest peaks

From this point on, the trail becomes narrower, steeper, darker, and rockier as you continue ascending Clinch Mountain to reach Middle Knob. At the 2.9-mile mark, stay left (again), this time for the marked Channels Spur Trail, but don't race to the top or you will miss one of the highlights of this hike—and it's exceptionally easy to miss. At the 3.0-mile mark, you will reach a bit of an intersection. There's a massive old fire tower and a rock scramble on the right. The tower is like a bright shiny object. You won't be able to look away, but you must. Turn left and walk as far as you can (it's not more than ten or fifteen steps). You will see a stack of rocks. Step up on the rocks, push the brush out of the way, then wow. Just wow. Get ready to be bowled over by the most incredible south-facing views. There are gigantic rocks to step out on to fully take in the vistas. From here, you can see both Mount Rogers and Whitetop Mountain, Virginia's two tallest peaks.

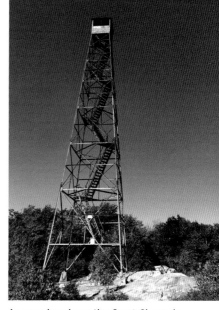

As you close in on the Great Channels, you'll reach a very large fire tower that leads to the trail that picks up on the other side of the tower.

Once you've soaked it all in, navigate back to the intersection in the trail, *then* walk toward the fire tower. You'll have to walk across a massive rock field, then go under or around the fire tower (you cannot climb this fire tower). The trail picks up on the other side as it ducks back into the now quite dense forest. In a few more steps, at the 3.3-mile mark, you will be in the sandstone maze, but don't rush in. Just before you enter, place a backpack or water bottle at the entrance before you explore. It is unbelievably easy to get turned around inside the maze. Then take your time navigating and snapping pictures through this sand-floored labyrinth that was created more than 10,000 years ago by ice wedging and permafrost. Once you've finished, retrace your steps to the trailhead. Your hike is complete at the 6.6-mile mark.

MILES AND DIRECTIONS

0.0 Begin at the small parking area for Channels Natural Area Preserve on VA 80.

0.2 Reach a turnoff on the right for Raven Ridge Lodge. Bypass this and stay to the left.

0.5 Arrive at a power-line vista on the left side of the trail.

0.6 The trail splits. Stay to the left.

2.9 Turn left onto the Channels Spur Trail.

3.0 Reach an intersection. Turn left and walk out onto the rocks for big views. Retrace your steps to the main trail.

3.1 Turn left and walk under the fire tower. The trail picks up on the other side of the tower.

3.3 Arrive at the Great Channels. Retrace your steps to the parking area.

6.6 Arrive back at the parking area. Your hike is complete.

28 MOLLY'S KNOB

This short, steep hike wows with views across Hungry Mother Lake, as well as gorgeous mountain vistas from one of the state's most beautiful overlooks.

Start: North of parking area on Lake Drive
Elevation gain: 994 feet
Distance: 3.6 miles out and back
Difficulty: Moderate
Hiking time: 2 to 3 hours
Best season: Year-round
Fees and permits: $$
Trail contact: Hungry Mother State Park, 2854 Park Blvd., Marion; (276) 781-7400; https://dcr.virginia.gov /state-parks/hungry-mother

Dogs: Yes
Trail surface: Mostly dirt and rock trails
Land status: State park
Nearest town: Marion
Maps: National Geographic Trails Illustrated Topographic Map 786 (Mount Rogers Recreation Area)
Amenities: Restrooms and in-season concessions at the lake beach
Maximum grade: 26%
Cell service: Fairly reliable

FINDING THE TRAILHEAD

The trailhead is located on the opposite side of Lake Drive, just north of the small parking area and south of the park's cabins. **GPS:** N36°53'09.5" / W81°31'16.0"

THE CLIMB

There's no question that the hike to Molly's Knob (elevation 3,245 feet) at Hungry Mother State Park in Marion leads to one of the most beautiful overlooks in the entire state. The views are beyond first-rate, but you'll have to earn them, particularly in the final steps on the Molly's Vista Trail. Get ready to dig deep and reap significant rewards when you arrive at the summit.

At the trailhead, you'll see a large trail kiosk and a trail marker leading you south along the white-blazed Molly's Knob Trail. A moderate ascent begins right away, but by the 0.3-mark you'll be able to take in views across 108-acre Hungry Mother Lake, which can be packed with splashing kids and families on warm summer days.

Continue on until you arrive at an observation deck with benches at the 0.4-mile mark. There's nothing to see here, but it is a well-shaded spot to catch your breath. Turn left here to stay on the Molly's Knob Trail. Keep climbing on this forested trail; you'll pass three small red benches on your way to the summit. Pay attention as you near the 1.4-mile mark, which is where you'll need to turn left for the purple-blazed Molly's Vista Trail. It's very easy to miss the sign (and all the big views).

To be candid, the Molly's Vista Trail will test you. It's just 0.4 mile, but it's much steeper than the Molly's Knob Trail. You'll really need to dig deep for this one, even with the switchbacks that help moderate the climb. Thankfully, one of the aforementioned

◄ Top: At the 0.4-mile mark, enjoy views across 108-acre Hungry Mother Lake.
Bottom: At the overlook, settle in on one of the benches and savor the gorgeous mountain views, including Mount Rogers and Whitetop Mountain.

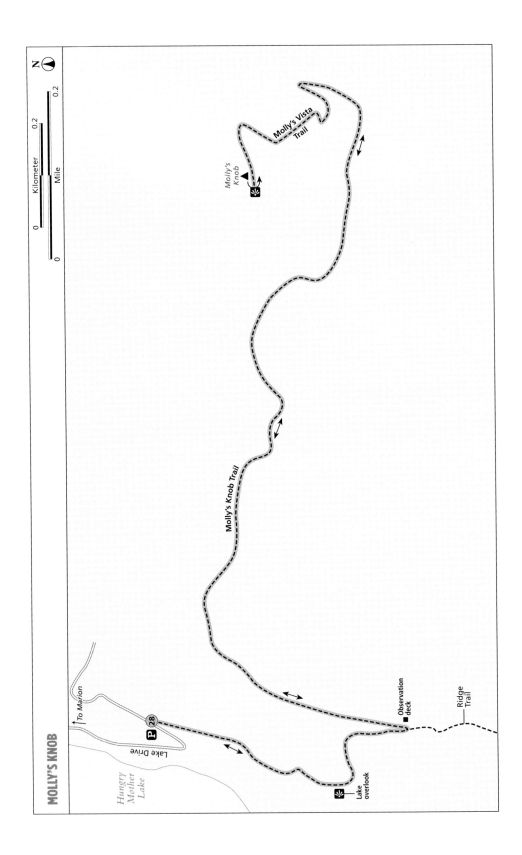

MOLLY'S KNOB

Hungry Mother Lake

To Marion

Lake Drive

P 28

Lake overlook

Observation deck

Ridge Trail

Molly's Knob Trail

Molly's Knob

Molly's Vista Trail

N

Kilometer
0   0.2

Mile
0   0.2

Several well-placed benches along the Molly's Knob Trail and Molly's Vista Trail allow you to take a seat and catch your breath on the way to the overlook.

red benches turns up at the 1.5-mile mark. Take a seat and catch your breath, but keep going. The overlook is close at hand. At the 1.8-mile mark, you will reach the top of Molly's Knob, where two more benches await to allow you to sit and savor the views across to Mount Rogers National Recreation Area, including Mount Rogers and White-top Mountain. Once you've reveled in the panoramic vistas, retrace your steps to the parking area. Your hike is complete at the 3.6-mile mark.

MILES AND DIRECTIONS

0.0 Begin at the large trail kiosk north of the parking area on Lake Drive.

0.3 Enjoy the views from above across Hungry Mother Lake.

0.4 Arrive at an observation deck. Turn left here to stay on the Molly's Knob Trail.

1.4 Veer left for the Molly's Vista Trail.

1.8 Reach the overlook. Retrace your steps to the parking area.

3.6 Arrive back at the parking area. Your hike is complete.

The hike to Molly's Knob begins at a trail kiosk just north of the parking area on Lake Drive.

29 MOUNT ROGERS

The hike to Mount Rogers may be light on views, but you'll be awed when you enter the mossy *Jurassic Park*–like spruce-fir forest in the final steps to the state's highpoint.

Start: Elk Garden parking area
Elevation gain: 1,778 feet
Distance: 9.0 miles out and back
Difficulty: Moderate
Hiking time: 4 to 5 hours
Best season: Year-round
Fees and permits: Free
Trail contact: George Washington and Jefferson National Forest (Mount Rogers National Recreation Area), 3714 Hwy. 16, Marion; (276) 783-5196; www.fs.usda.gov/detail /gwj
Dogs: Yes

Trail surface: Mostly dirt and rock trails
Land status: National forest
Nearest town: Chilhowie
Maps: National Geographic Trails Illustrated Topographic Map 1503 (Appalachian Trail: Damascus to Bailey Gap) and Map 318 (Mount Rogers High Country)
Amenities: Vault toilet in parking area
Maximum grade: 16%
Cell service: Fairly reliable

FINDING THE TRAILHEAD

The trailhead is located across Whitetop Road (VA 600) from the Elk Garden parking area, which has room for more than a dozen cars to comfortably park. There is also a vault toilet and a large trail map in the lot. **GPS:** N36°38'47.2" / W81°35'00.4"

THE CLIMB

A guide to summit hikes in Virginia would be incomplete without a trek to the state's highpoint, Mount Rogers (elevation 5,729 feet). However, let's get this out of the way now: There is no view from the summit. It's completely closed in by dense forest. However, that's not to say there's no reason to complete this hike. In fact, there's a lot to love about this forested hike to the top of Mount Rogers, including curious cows, grassy highlands, and a unique spruce-fir ecosystem.

There are two ways to reach the summit of Mount Rogers, and both are out-and-back hikes that clock in at 9.0 miles. Here, we're covering the northbound approach on the white-blazed Appalachian Trail, which is a well-shaded and less-trafficked route. The parking lot is also free. The southbound approach begins at Grayson Highlands State Park, so a per-vehicle daily parking fee is required.

Once you cross over Whitetop Road, go through the gate that keeps in the cattle, then proceed along the Appalachian Trail. Within the first few steps, a wooden trail sign nudges you to the left to stay on the trail. The first 0.5 mile is a mild ascent across open grassland where you'll see cows grazing alongside the trail. You'll then enjoy the

Top: Your efforts are rewarded at the 3.0-mile mark when you reach an overlook ▶ across the grassy highlands that's just steps from the Appalachian Trail.
Bottom: As you close in on Mount Rogers, you enter a spruce-fir forest with plenty of moss-draped logs and lush green ferns alongside the blue-blazed Mount Rogers Trail.

The summit of Mount Rogers is largely closed in by forest, but a cluster of large rocks let you know you have reached the top of the mountain.

shade of the forest as you enter the Lewis Fork Wilderness within the Jefferson National Forest.

From here, you're walking through a dense hardwood forest. It's very quiet and relaxing. At the 2.0-mile mark is a large trail sign. You'll be relieved to know that you are still going in the right direction, and that Mount Rogers is just 2.5 miles farther up the trail. You can also turn right here for a spur trail to a spring or to connect with the Virginia Highlands Horse Trail. In a few more steps, you'll reach a switchback and a trail junction at the 2.1-mile mark. Make a hard right uphill to stay on the southbound section of the Appalachian Trail.

As you climb, you'll encounter a couple of sets of stone steps built into the trail, then a much-deserved reward at the 3.0-mile mark as the forest opens up to reveal a gorgeous lookout across the grassy highlands. Take in the open balds and lush meadows, but then keep moving. You'll be out of the woods for good—for now—at the 3.7-mile mark. Savor the wide-open views. You may even pass a campsite or two as the area is quite popular with backpackers.

At the 3.9-mile mark, you'll reach the blue-blazed Mount Rogers Trail. Turn left here and continue the ascent, which leads you back into the forest. You may soon begin to feel as though you've been dropped into *Jurassic Park*. The trail all of a sudden becomes mossy, much like a temperate rain forest. In fact, you have now entered a spruce-fir forest, a rare ecosystem that only exists in the Southern Appalachian region at elevations greater

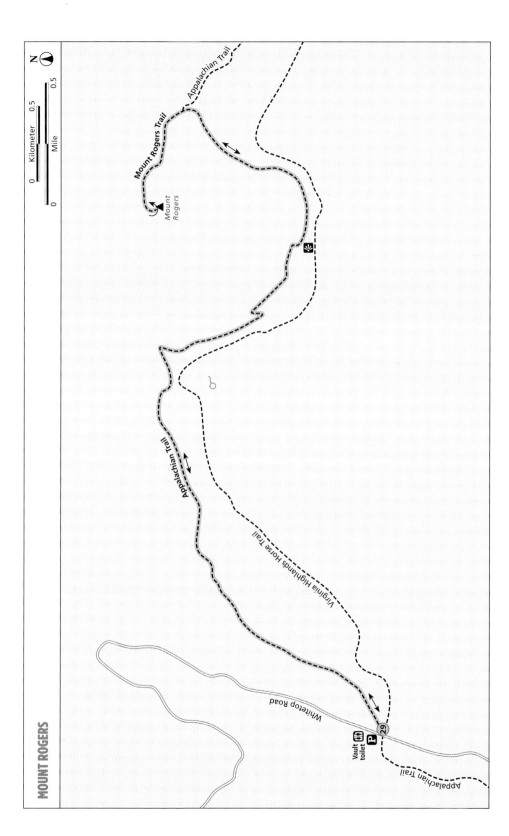

MOUNT ROGERS

N

Kilometer
0   0.5

Mile
0   0.5

Appalachian Trail

Mount Rogers Trail

Mount Rogers

Appalachian Trail

Virginia Highlands Horse Trail

Whitetop Road

Vault toilet
P
29

Appalachian Trail

There's not much in the way of views from atop Mount Rogers, but keep your eyes open for the survey marker that marks the highpoint of Virginia.

than 5,500 feet, where the cold climate cannot support the broad-leaved hardwood forest found at lower elevations. Moss drapes across fallen logs and free-standing trees, while lush ferns carpet swaths of the forest floor.

You will reach the summit at the 4.5-mile mark. Only a couple of large rocks and a survey marker indicate the state's highpoint. Still, it's quite an accomplishment to reach the highpoint of Virginia, so take time to celebrate. From the summit, retrace your steps to the Elk Garden parking area. Your hike is complete at the 9.0-mile mark.

MILES AND DIRECTIONS

0.0 Begin on the southbound stretch of the white-blazed Appalachian Trail, which picks up across Whitetop Road from the Elk Garden parking area.

0.5 Enter the Lewis Fork Wilderness.

2.1 Turn right to stay on the southbound Appalachian Trail.

3.0 Arrive at an overlook for views across the grassy highlands.

3.9 Turn left on the blue-blazed Mount Rogers Trail.

4.5 Reach the summit of Mount Rogers. Retrace your steps to the parking area.

9.0 Arrive back at the parking lot. Your hike is complete.

30 WHITE ROCKS

Hike to the top of what was once a guiding beacon for westward-bound settlers, on the far east end of Cumberland Gap National Historical Park.

Start: Civic Park parking area
Elevation gain: 2,277 feet
Distance: 8.1-mile lollipop
Difficulty: Moderate
Hiking time: 5 to 6 hours
Best season: Year-round
Fees and permits: Free
Trail contact: Cumberland Gap National Historical Park, 91 Bartlett Park Rd., Middlesboro, KY; (606) 248-2817; www.nps.gov/cuga/

Dogs: Yes
Trail surface: Mostly dirt and rock trails, some paved trails
Land status: National historical park
Nearest town: Cumberland Gap
Maps: Park map available at www.nps.gov/cuga/
Amenities: Restrooms
Maximum grade: 33%
Cell service: Fairly reliable

FINDING THE TRAILHEAD

The trailhead is located at the parking area for Civic Park on Civitan Park Road. There are a dozen or so parking spaces, as well as vault toilets and a picnic shelter. **GPS:** N36°39'07.8" / W83°26'08.2"

THE CLIMB

There's so much to love about this hike, well beyond the far-reaching views across three states—Tennessee, Virginia, and Kentucky. The overlook vistas at White Rocks (elevation 3,343 feet) are incredible, but this 8.1-mile hike on the far east end of Cumberland Gap National Historical Park will wow you on many levels.

As you walk toward the trailhead for the Ewing Trail, you will see three colorful signs educating visitors on Cumberland Gap, including White Rocks, which was a guiding beacon for westbound settlers from 1775 to 1810. The hiking trail begins just past the signs, first as a paved trail, then as a mostly dirt and rock path.

At the 0.5-mile mark, turn left onto the Ewing Trail, a multiuse trail that is shared with horseback riders. From here, the hike is a slow, shaded ascent through eastern deciduous forest. You will see a sign for White Rocks at the 2.3-mile mark. Bypass this sign and continue on the Ewing Trail. You'd be remiss if you did not make an exploration of Sand Cave a part of your hike. You will have time to see White Rocks on the other side of this moderate lollipop hike.

You will reach a T-junction at the 3.5-mile mark. Turn right for the Ridge Trail. You'll then reach a spur trail, as well as a hitching post (as in, no horses are allowed past this point), at the 3.7-mile mark. From here, you're a short 0.2 mile from Sand Cave, a 250-foot-wide half-dome cave filled with an acre of beach-like sand. In the final steps, you'll descend more than 100 feet, including down a wooden ladder, before you are greeted by a trickling waterfall just left of the cave. After a good rain, there can be an impressive flow at this waterfall. At the 3.9-mile mark, you have arrived at the massive and awe-inspiring cave.

It's a rather steep climb into the cave across what feels like a sand dune, but it's a must to trek to the very back of the cave to snap a photo of the cave opening. The hiking trail is in Virginia, but the actual cave is in Kentucky, so both states claim this spectacular natural wonder as their own. Once you've taken in all the glory of this cave, retrace your steps to the Ridge Trail, then turn left to continue on.

At the 5.0-mile mark, you will see a trail sign for White Rocks as well as hitching posts. Horses are not permitted on the narrow 0.3-mile stretch of trail that leads to the top of White Rocks. It's a short walk to the overlook, but the last 100 yards are rather steep. Thankfully, the gorgeous south-facing views serve as a worthy reward for the short but strenuous climb. Enjoy a snack, soak up the views, and rehydrate before continuing on to complete this hike.

◀ Top: You'll descend more than 100 feet, on foot and by way of a wooden ladder, in the final approach to Sand Cave.

Bottom: Get ready to be awed by the 250-foot-wide Sand Cave near the middle of this lollipop hike to White Rocks in Southwest Virginia.

Retrace your steps, then turn left onto a connector trail at the 5.6-mile mark that indicates the route back to the parking area. This downhill trail connects with the Ewing Trail at the 5.8-mile mark; this is the trail you bypassed at the 2.3-mile mark to hike to Sand Cave. It was worth it, right? Turn left once you reach the Ewing Trail, then retrace your steps to the parking area. Your hike is complete at the 8.1-mile mark.

MILES AND DIRECTIONS

0.0 Begin at the trailhead in the parking area for Civic Park.

0.5 Turn left onto the Ewing Trail.

2.3 Reach a junction with a sign for White Rocks. Continue on the Ewing Trail.

3.5 Arrive at a T-junction. Turn right for the Ridge Trail.

3.7 Turn left onto a connector trail for Sand Cave.

3.9 Arrive at Sand Cave. Retrace your steps to the Ridge Trail, then turn left.

5.0 Reach a sign for a spur trail to White Rocks.

5.3 Arrive at White Rocks. Retrace your steps to the start of the spur trail.

5.6 Turn left onto a connector trail that leads to the Ewing Trail.

5.8 Turn left onto the Ewing Trail.

8.1 Arrive back at the parking area. Your hike is complete.

OPTION

If you would like a more direct route to White Rocks, turn right from the Ewing Trail at the sign for White Rocks at the 2.3-mile mark. At the 2.5-mile mark, turn right again for White Rocks. You will arrive at the overlook at the 2.8-mile mark. Soak up the views, take a few sips of water, then retrace your steps to the parking area for a 5.6-mile out-and-back hike.

◀ Top: Soak up all the south-facing views from the rocky overlook at the top of White Rocks.
Bottom: Get ready for big views from the overlook atop White Rocks, the one-time beacon that guided westward-bound settlers to the historic Cumberland Gap.

VIRGINIA MOUNTAINS

While Southwest Virginia is a gorgeous natural playground, the breathtaking region is quite a drive for many in the state. From Roanoke—which many consider to be Southwest Virginia—it can be another 3 to 4 hours in the car to reach some areas that are deep in the state's Heart of Appalachia region. A closer-in alternative is the Virginia Mountains region, which is anchored by Roanoke in the Blue Ridge Mountains.

This mountainous region is a mecca for outdoor enthusiasts, including those who love to fish, paddle, bike, and hike. The Appalachian Trail and the Blue Ridge Parkway (more than 200 miles of this scenic byway meander through Virginia) slice through the southern section of this region. In the north, the Appalachian Mountains and George Washington and Jefferson National Forest welcome hikers of all levels.

The spectacular Virginia Mountains region is home to two of the state's bucket list hiking trifectas. The first is Virginia's Triple Crown in Catawba, which includes Cove Mountain (Dragon's Tooth), Tinker Mountain (Tinker Cliffs), and McAfee Knob. The latter is widely considered to be the most photographed protrusion on the entire Appalachian Trail. These hikes can be done individually, or you can tack them together by way of extra sections of the Appalachian Trail. This 34-mile loop is especially popular with backpackers. The second is the three Peaks of Otter in Bedford. These three hikes include Sharp Top, Flat Top, and Harkening Hill. Sharp Top is the most popular, especially with early-morning sunrise-seekers.

Every hike in this section has so much to offer summit hikers, such as far-reaching views and plenty of companionship from fellow hikers eager to check off trifecta hikes and bucket list–worthy treks to the top of breathtaking mountains.

◀ The 35-foot-tall rock spire called Dragon's Tooth is as magnificent in person as it is in photos.

31 APPLE ORCHARD MOUNTAIN

This easy hike starts on the Blue Ridge Parkway near Bedford and leads to big views from both the Thunder Ridge Overlook and Apple Orchard Mountain.

Start: Thunder Ridge parking area
Elevation gain: 925 feet
Distance: 5.3 miles out and back
Difficulty: Easy
Hiking time: 3 to 4 hours
Best season: Year-round
Fees and permits: Free
Trail contact: George Washington and Jefferson National Forest (Glenwood-Pedlar Ranger District), 27 Ranger Ln., Natural Bridge Station; (540) 291-2188; www.fs.usda .gov/detail/gwj

Dogs: Yes
Trail surface: Mostly dirt and gravel trails, some stone steps
Land status: National forest
Nearest town: Buena Vista
Maps: National Geographic Trails Illustrated Topographic Map 789 (Lexington, Blue Ridge Mountains)
Amenities: Picnic table
Maximum grade: 26% (stone steps)
Cell service: Reliable

FINDING THE TRAILHEAD

 The trailhead is located at the back of the large Thunder Ridge parking area at milepost 74.7 on the Blue Ridge Parkway. **GPS:** N37°32'24.3" / W79°29'24.8"

THE CLIMB

In this book, there are some very steep hikes, like Elliott Knob and Big House Mountain, but a hike doesn't have to be steep or have a ruthless elevation gain to awe with wide-open views. The hike to Apple Orchard Mountain near Bedford is just such a hike. Even better, this out-and-back hike along the white-blazed Appalachian Trail wows with double the views. The first vista is just steps from the Thunder Ridge parking area on the Blue Ridge Parkway. The Thunder Ridge Overlook boasts 180-degree views for miles and miles across the Arnold Valley. The second view is from the top of Apple Orchard Mountain (elevation 4,225 feet), where you can enjoy south-facing vistas from a rocky outcrop that's adjacent to a large, grassy clearing. It can be easy to miss if you're head-down focused on your steps and the trail.

From the parking area, pause to revel in the dramatic vistas from the stone overlook at Thunder Ridge. From here, continue south along the Appalachian Trail. There are some ups and downs, but overall it's a well-maintained stretch of forested trail in the Jefferson National Forest. You'll cross over the Blue Ridge Parkway at the 0.4-mile mark and then arrive at a sign for the Thunder Hill Shelter in another mile, at the 1.4-mile mark. Turn left here. It's a very short walk to this lean-to hikers' shelter, which also has a picnic table, stone fire pit, and bear box (for locking away smell-ables, like food, trash, and lotions).

◀ Top: Just steps from the start of this hike is the Thunder Ridge Overlook, a stone viewing platform that wows with views for miles across the Arnold Valley.

Bottom: A short spur trail leads to the Thunder Hill Shelter, a common lean-to hikers' shelter that can be found along the Appalachian Trail.

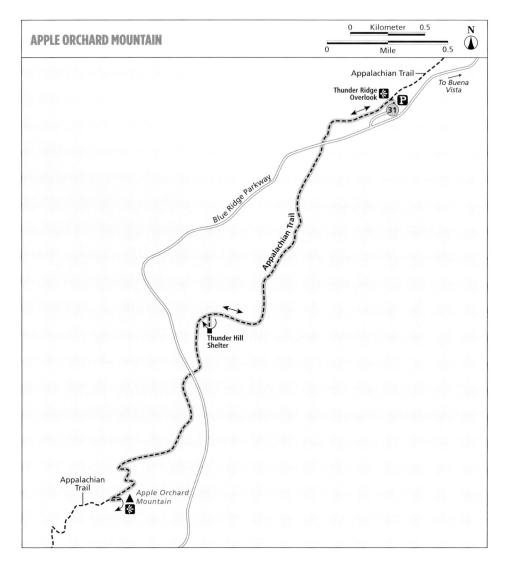

Once you've explored the shelter area, retrace your steps, then continue south on the Appalachian Trail.

You'll cross back over the Blue Ridge Parkway at the 1.8-mile mark. Then get ready for the generally mild trail to get more rocky, but not to worry, it's nothing too serious. However, you will see a massive rock wedged in between two square-like boulders. Just under the rock is a set of stone steps, which make you wonder whether this oddity is natural or man-made. As you proceed, you'll reach more stone steps built into the trail, then a large clearing at the 2.6-mile mark, as well as a sizable soccer ball–like radar tower. Today this is an FAA long-range radar tower that tracks aircraft activity. Up until 1975, this dome was Bedford Air Force Station.

When you reach a curiously large boulder wedged between two square-like ▶ rock slabs, you'll have to wonder whether it's a natural or man-made oddity.

Tucked away behind a grove of evergreens atop Apple Orchard Mountain is a rocky outcrop that inspires with views across the Blue Ridge Mountains.

From the clearing, you can catch some views to the north and south. However, you need to hunt a bit for the big views, the views you've hiked all this way to see. Keep your eyes on a small grove of evergreens on the left side of the trail. Just past the evergreens is a rocky outcrop with magnificent south-facing vistas. There is also a weathered sign trumpeting that this is, in fact, Apple Orchard Mountain. You did it. Once you've soaked in all the views, retrace your steps to the parking area. Your hike is complete at the parking area at the 5.3-mile mark.

MILES AND DIRECTIONS

0.0 Begin on a connector trail at the back of the Thunder Ridge parking area on the Blue Ridge Parkway at milepost 74.7.

0.1 Stop to take in the views at the Thunder Ridge Overlook. Begin hiking south on the Appalachian Trail.

0.4 Cross the Blue Ridge Parkway.

1.4 Turn left to walk to the Thunder Hill Shelter. Retrace your steps to the Appalachian Trail, then turn left to continue on.

1.8 Cross back over the Blue Ridge Parkway.

2.6 Reach a grassy clearing. A soccer ball–like radar tower is on the left. Just behind a small grove of evergreens is a rocky overlook for vistas from atop Apple Orchard Mountain. Take in the views, then retrace your steps to the parking area.

5.3 Arrive back at the parking area. Your hike is complete.

32 BALD KNOB

This short out-and-back hike can be a real slog at times, but the views from the summit of Bald Knob are worth every ounce of your efforts.

Start: Trailhead on Bald Knob Road
Elevation gain: 410 feet
Distance: 1.0 mile out and back
Difficulty: Moderate
Hiking time: 45 to 90 minutes
Best season: Year-round
Fees and permits: Free
Trail contact: Mountain Lake Conservancy, 115 Hotel Circle, Pembroke; (540) 626-7121; www.mtnlakelodge.com/preserve /conservancy

Dogs: Yes
Trail surface: Mostly dirt and rock trails
Land status: Wilderness conservancy area
Nearest town: Pembroke
Maps: National Geographic Trails Illustrated Topographic Map 787 (Blacksburg, New River Valley)
Amenities: None
Maximum grade: 28%
Cell service: Unreliable

FINDING THE TRAILHEAD

The trailhead is located on Bald Knob Road, a gravel road just south of Mountain Lake Lodge. Note that the parking lot is on Mountain Lake Road, adjacent to Mountain Lake Outfitters. **GPS:** N37°21'15.5" / W80°32'17.7"

THE CLIMB

There are at least two Bald Knobs in Virginia. It seems to be a fairly popular name for a knob, which by the way is defined by *Merriam-Webster's* as "a rounded usually isolated hill or mountain." This guidebook includes eight hike-worthy knobs in Virginia. This Bald Knob (elevation 4,354 feet), the one in Pembroke, is a favorite among Virginia Tech students eager to get off campus and savor a vibrantly colored sunset from the rocky summit. In fact, the trailhead is a short 25-minute drive from the university.

The Bald Knob Trail is located on the grounds of Mountain Lake Lodge. Some may know this property better by its on-screen name: Kellerman's. Yes, this is the lodge where the Housemans summered in the 1987 movie *Dirty Dancing*. You'll see paraphernalia and placards with "movie moments" around the property. The inside dining room looks just as it does in the movie.

There are two ways to the top of Bald Knob. Both are rather steep but well worth the climb for the far-reaching mountain views, especially at sunset. The easier, though steeper, way is via a 1.0-mile out-and-back hike. Yes, it's just 0.5 mile to the summit, but you'll encounter a fairly stiff elevation gain of more than 400 feet on the way up. There are a couple of switchbacks to help numb the pain, but it's pretty much a schlepp for this view.

From Bald Knob Road, ascend the narrow Bald Knob Trail. In 0.4 mile, you'll reach steps to climb for Salt Pond Mountain. You'll also see a sign for the Cliff Trail. Ignore this sign or you will miss the overlook at Bald Knob completely. It's rather confusing.

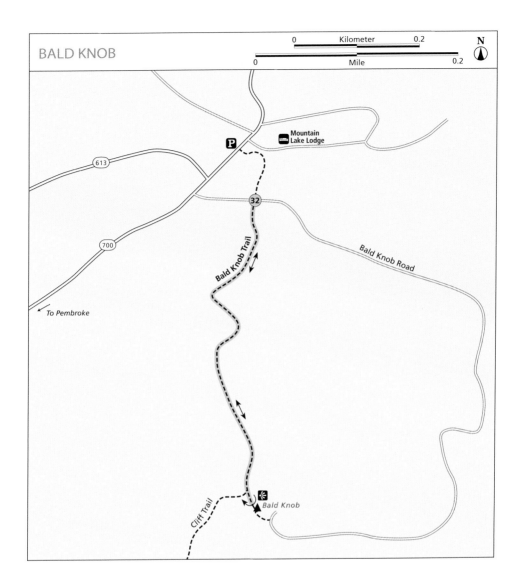

At the 0.5-mile mark, catch your breath. You have arrived at the overlook. There are lots of rocky outcrops to sit on and savor the perfectly west-facing views. There's room for everyone, but there's even more space if you continue past the left-most rock. A hidden trail leads off to the left to reveal more wide-open flat rocks and stunningly beautiful views.

Once you've taken in every view and the sun has dipped below the horizon, retrace your steps to return to the lodge. It will be dark in the dense forest, so bring along a headlamp for an illuminated and hands-free descent back to the trailhead and the lodge.

◄ Top: You may recognize Mountain Lake Lodge. Its screen name is Kellerman's. It's the main lodge from the 1987 film, *Dirty Dancing*.

Bottom: You won't see any painted trail blazes on the Bald Knob Trail, but there is fairly good signage along the way to keep you going in the right direction.

A short but steep hike leads to the summit of Bald Knob, where hardy hikers can sit and savor perfectly west-facing sunset views.

MILES AND DIRECTIONS

0.0 Begin at the trailhead on Bald Knob Road.

0.4 Arrive at and ascend steps to reach the summit and overlook.

0.5 Reach the summit. Sit and savor the views. There are plenty of flat rocks. Retrace your steps to the trailhead.

1.0 Arrive back at the trailhead. Your hike is complete.

OPTION

As an alternative to an out-and-back hike, you can tackle the climb to the top of Bald Knob as a 1.6-mile loop. For this hike, ascend the gravel Bald Knob Road. You'll pass several trail signs on the way, but keep on going. At the 0.6-mile mark, turn left to stay on this gravel road. Just past the 0.9-mile mark, you'll see a sign on the left for the Homestead Trail, which actually sets off to the right, starting with some stone steps. In another 0.2 mile you'll arrive at the overlook. Once you've soaked it all in, look for a wooden sign for the Bald Knob Trail to descend to Bald Knob Road to complete your hike.

33 COVE MOUNTAIN

This hike requires a technical rock scramble, but the rewards are substantial when you reach the dramatic 35-foot-tall spire called Dragon's Tooth at the top of Cove Mountain in Catawba.

Start: Parking area on Catawba Valley Drive
Elevation gain: 1,309 feet
Distance: 4.8 miles out and back
Difficulty: Strenuous
Hiking time: 3 to 4 hours
Best season: Year-round
Fees and permits: Free
Trail contact: George Washington and Jefferson National Forest (Eastern Divide Ranger District), 110 Southpark Dr., Blacksburg; (540) 552-4641; www.fs.usda.gov /detail/gwj

Dogs: Yes
Trail surface: Mostly dirt and rock trails
Land status: National forest
Nearest town: Salem
Maps: National Geographic's Trails Illustrated Topographic Map 1504 (Appalachian Trail: Bailey Gap to Calf Mountain)
Amenities: Vault toilet
Maximum grade: 30%
Cell service: Reliable

FINDING THE TRAILHEAD

The trailhead is located at the back of the large parking area on Catawba Valley Drive. If you get shut out from the lot—this is a very popular hike—there are plenty of legal spots for parallel parking. **GPS:** N37°22'42.5" / W80°09'21.5"

THE CLIMB

Some know this hike in Catawba as Cove Mountain (elevation 3,025 feet), but it's more popularly known as Dragon's Tooth, so nicknamed for its 35-foot-tall rock spire at the summit. It's one part of the trifecta of bucket-list hikes in the Roanoke Valley called Virgina's Triple Crown (the other two hikes are McAfee Knob and Tinker Cliffs).

From the trailhead, your first steps are on the blue-blazed Dragon's Tooth Trail. At the 0.2-mile mark, stay right to bypass the Boy Scout Trail, then get ready to hopscotch across four or five water crossings, cross over a few wooden footbridges, and traverse several stepping-stone paths that nicely break up a relatively straightforward hike through the densely forested woods.

It's a gradual climb along the Dragon's Tooth Trail until you reach a caution sign at the 1.5-mile mark, politely informing you that the next mile of trail is "rocky and steep." In a few more steps, you'll see a sign for Lost Spectacles Gap. It's here that the Dragon's Tooth Trail dead-ends and becomes the white-blazed Appalachian Trail. You'll closely follow the southbound section of trail for the next 0.7 mile, but it's not going to be a walk in the park. More like a rocky climb up a mountain. As you turn right, the trail takes a turn literally and figuratively as this section becomes decidedly more technical and strenuous.

There are steep, rocky steps, even areas that make you feel as though you're scaling the side of Cove Mountain, thanks in part to iron bars to grab hold of to climb open rock faces. Secure your water bottle and phone. Put your hiking poles away. You'll want full access to your hands, knees, feet, and elbows to scramble to the top from here on. Once

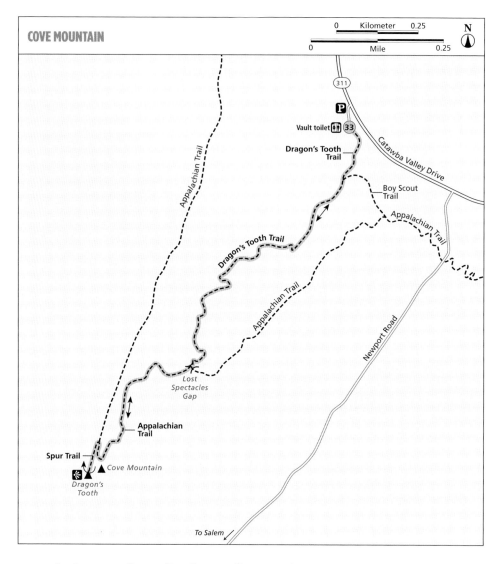

0   Kilometer   0.25

0   Mile   0.25

N

311

Vault toilet 33

Dragon's Tooth
Trail

Catawba Valley Drive

Appalachian Trail

Boy Scout
Trail

Dragon's Tooth Trail

Appalachian Trail

Appalachian Trail

Newport Road

Lost
Spectacles
Gap

Appalachian
Trail

Spur Trail

Cove Mountain

Dragon's
Tooth

To Salem

you are back on terra firma—literally—you'll see a trail sign. Turn left for a blue-blazed spur trail that leads to Dragon's Tooth. From here, it's a short 0.1-mile stroll to big views. Pat yourself on the back. You made it to the top.

The dramatic 35-foot-tall spire is out of this world. It's just, wow. Seriously. There's an open area as you approach Dragon's Tooth (also called The Tooth) where you can settle in on a small rock to rehydrate and collect yourself after the climb. There are plenty of fantastic views across the Roanoke Valley from this level. However, an intrepid few may also wish to climb to the top of the spire for even more breathtaking mountain vistas. Soak it all in, then retrace your steps to the parking area. Your hike is complete at the 4.8-mile mark.

You'll need full access to hands, knees, elbows, and feet for a ▶
rock climb as you close in on the summit of Cove Mountain.

Early in this hike, you'll hopscotch across gently flowing streams and tiptoe across large stepping-stones built into the Dragon's Tooth Trail.

MILES AND DIRECTIONS

0.0 Begin at the back of the parking area, on the blue-blazed Dragon's Tooth Trail.

0.2 Stay to the right to continue on the Dragon's Tooth Trail.

1.5 The Dragon's Tooth Trail ends. Turn right for the Appalachian Trail.

2.3 Turn left onto a blue-blazed spur trail to Dragon's Tooth.

2.4 Reach the Dragon's Tooth. Retrace your steps to the parking area.

4.8 Arrive back at the parking area. Your hike is complete.

Whether you choose to climb to the top of the spire or stick to the rocky outcrops at the base, you'll be bowled over by the views across the Roanoke Valley.

34 **FLAT TOP**

This steep, forested hike leads to multiple outcrops for big views from the top of Flat Top, the tallest of the three Peaks of Otter in Bedford.

Start: Parking area on Blue Ridge Parkway
Elevation gain: 1,752 feet
Distance: 5.7 miles out and back
Difficulty: Moderate
Hiking time: 3 to 4 hours
Best season: Year-round
Fees and permits: Free
Trail contact: Peaks of Otter Visitor Center, 85919 Blue Ridge Parkway, Bedford; (540) 586-4496; www.nps .gov/blri/

Dogs: Yes
Trail surface: Mostly dirt and rock trails
Land status: National park (Blue Ridge Parkway)
Nearest town: Bedford
Maps: National Geographic Trails Illustrated Topographic Map 789 (Lexington, Blue Ridge Mountains)
Amenities: None
Maximum grade: 32%
Cell service: Spotty

FINDING THE TRAILHEAD

Use the trailhead that starts at the parking area (space for at least a dozen vehicles) on the east side of the Blue Ridge Parkway at milepost 83. **GPS:** N37°28'06.3" / W79°34'49.7"

THE CLIMB

Flat Top is one of three rugged mountains that make up the Peaks of Otter in Bedford. At an elevation of 4,001 feet, it's the tallest of the three hike-worthy trifecta peaks along the Blue Ridge Parkway. There are two routes to the summit of Flat Top, both of which guide hikers along the Flat Top Trail. The westbound hike (5.7 miles out and back) originates from a parking area at milepost 83 on the Blue Ridge Parkway. Meanwhile, the eastbound hike (4.7 miles out and back) begins southeast of Abbott Lake and requires that you park and start your hike at Peaks of Otter Lodge. Both hikes are roughly the same challenge-wise and are equally popular, though some may opt for the Abbott Lake route given the slightly shorter distance.

Here we're covering the westbound hike, which is sometimes called the Pinnacle Route given you pass a Pinnacle on the way to Flat Top. From the lot, you'll see the Flat Top Trail lead into the woods. From the get-go, you are ascending Flat Top Mountain. The trail runs parallel to the Blue Ridge Parkway for the first 0.7 mile as you climb 250 feet. If you listen, you can hear cars motoring along the scenic byway, but you may be more focused on your breathing. Thankfully, you will reach a rustic wooden bench at the 0.7-mile mark when you approach the first switchback in the hiking trail.

From here, you'll encounter several more switchbacks as you continue ascending Flat Top Mountain, then another bench and a massive rock at the 1.5-mile mark. At the 2.1-mile mark, you will arrive at a rocky outcrop for views (essentially, a false summit) and a sign noting that Cross Rock is just 0.1 mile down a spur trail. A very steep spur trail. Cross Rock is an interesting balanced rock formation that's in the shape of a cross. While 0.1 mile does not seem like much, it feels like more when you're climbing back up to the Flat Top Trail. It's cool to check out, but only if you have the time and energy *after* you

After you ascend 0.7 mile, a small wooden bench is a welcome sight at the corner of the first switchback on the Flat Top Trail.

Since the top of Flat Top is—not surprisingly—flat, some hikers walk right on by the summit. Thankfully, a sign lets hikers know that they have arrived at the summit.

make it to Flat Top. In a few more steps, you'll see the unmarked Pinnacle on the left. It's not incredibly obvious, so it's easy to miss.

The switchbacks end at the 2.1-mile mark. You will definitely want them back, too, because the last 0.6 mile to the top of Flat Top Mountain is a toughie. Thankfully, once you reach the top you are greeted with a sign marking the summit. Some people actually miss the summit because it's flat and therefore does not feel like a summit. However, there are multiple lookout points atop Flat Top. You just need to poke around to find them. You can even enjoy near 360-degree views, but not all from one place. You'll need to hop around to different overlooks.

From the summit, the Flat Top Trail continues but on to Abbott Lake, so be extra sure you retrace your steps and descend the mountain by way of the proper route. Otherwise, you may find yourself a good distance from your car and in need of a ride-share to drive you back to your parking lot. Your hike is complete at the 5.7-mile mark.

MILES AND DIRECTIONS

0.0 Begin from the parking area at milepost 83 on the Blue Ridge Parkway.

0.7 Arrive at the first switchback, as well as a wooden bench.

1.5 Reach a second wooden bench.

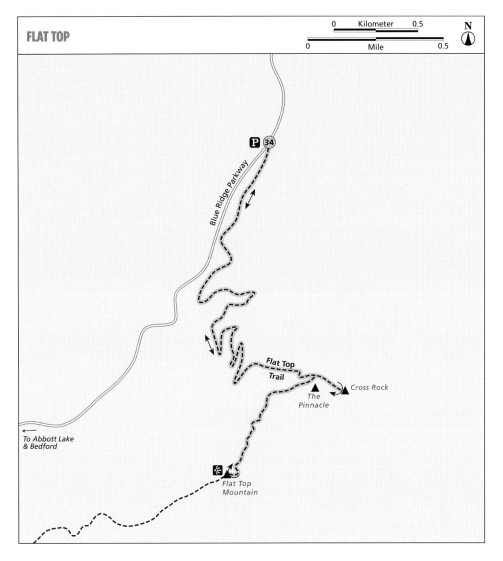

0   Kilometer   0.5

0   Mile   0.5

N

Blue Ridge Parkway

Flat Top Trail

The Pinnacle

Cross Rock

To Abbott Lake
& Bedford

Flat Top
Mountain

2.1   Arrive at a rocky outcrop for mountain views (false summit). Bypass (for now) a spur trail to Cross Rock.

2.7   Reach Flat Top. Hop around to different overlooks to enjoy the views. Retrace your steps.

3.4   Turn right onto the spur trail for Cross Rock.

3.5   Arrive at Cross Rock. Retrace your steps to the Flat Top Trail.

3.6   Reach the Flat Top Trail. Turn right to continue descending to the parking area.

5.7   Arrive back at the parking area. Your hike is complete.

Several rocky outcrops at the top of Flat Top allow hikers to take in the views across the Blue Ridge Mountains in multiple directions.

OPTION

The shorter 4.7-mile out-and-back hike to Flat Top begins from the parking area for the Peaks of Otter Lodge. Walk east along the paved Abbott Trail, then exit left onto a side trail for Polly Wood's Ordinary, a historic log cabin at the end of a service road for picnickers off Peaks Road. From here, walk 0.4 mile to the start of the northbound section of the Flat Top Trail. You will then climb more than 1,600 feet in elevation to reach the summit of Flat Top.

35 HARKENING HILL

This hike leads to the top of the smallest and most underrated of the three Peaks of Otter, but don't let that keep you from this climb. The summit views across the Blue Ridge Mountains are nothing short of spectacular.

Start: Peaks of Otter Visitor Center parking lot
Elevation gain: 876 feet
Distance: 3.5-mile loop
Difficulty: Moderate
Hiking time: 2 to 2.5 hours
Best season: Year-round
Fees and permits: Free
Trail contact: Peaks of Otter Visitor Center, 85919 Blue Ridge Parkway, Bedford; (540) 586-4496; www.nps.gov/blri/
Dogs: Yes

Trail surface: Mostly dirt and rock trails, some stone steps
Land status: National park (Blue Ridge Parkway)
Nearest town: Bedford
Maps: National Geographic Trails Illustrated Topographic Map 789 (Lexington, Blue Ridge Mountains)
Amenities: Flush toilets, visitor center
Maximum grade: 22%
Cell service: Spotty

FINDING THE TRAILHEAD

The hike begins at the east end of the parking area for the Peaks of Otter Visitor Center, at milepost 85.6 on the Blue Ridge Parkway. **GPS:** N37°26′53.5″ / W79°36′22.2″

THE CLIMB

At an elevation of 3,364 feet, Harkening Hill may be the smallest of the three Peaks of Otter in Bedford, but it's definitely much more than a hill. This underrated mountain is also well worth your time, not only because you'll encounter fewer fellow hikers—they're all across the Blue Ridge Parkway at Sharp Top, the most popular of the three peaks—but because the summit views are phenomenal. This is no also-ran mountain hike.

The hike begins and ends at the Peaks of Otter Visitor Center. There are three ways to complete this summit climb. For this option, from the east end of the parking area, head east on an easy walking path. You'll reach a trail sign at the 0.3-mile mark. Turn left here for the Johnson Trail, which slowly guides you up a forested hill. Er, mountain.

You won't actually see the trail name, Johnson Trail, on the trail, so walk in the direction of Harkening Hill. Near the 0.8-mile mark, you'll see another sign, directing you to turn left to continue on to Balance Rock and Harkening Hill (Harkening Hill Trail). At the 1.0-mile mark, you'll reach an open clearing. There are no trail markers, so just follow the matted grass until you reenter the forest and reconnect with the Johnson Trail.

At the 1.5-mile mark, you'll see a trail sign and a spur trail. Turn left here and descend 300 feet until you reach Balance Rock, a rather engaging rock formation. It does, in fact, look like a large rock balancing on top of another large rock. Some will say it's worthy of

HARKENING HILL LOOP TRAIL

SUMMIT

(ROOFT)

JOHNSON FARM

BALANCE ROCK

0.6 MILE

(1400 FEET)

(0.3 MILE)

BLUE RIDGE PARKWAY

YOU ARE HERE

TRAIL LEGEND

HARKENING HILL LOOP TRAIL
TOTAL LENGTH .33 MILES

ELK RUN TRAIL
TOTAL LENGTH .5 MILES

VISITOR CENTER

1300 FEET

RESTAURANT LODGE

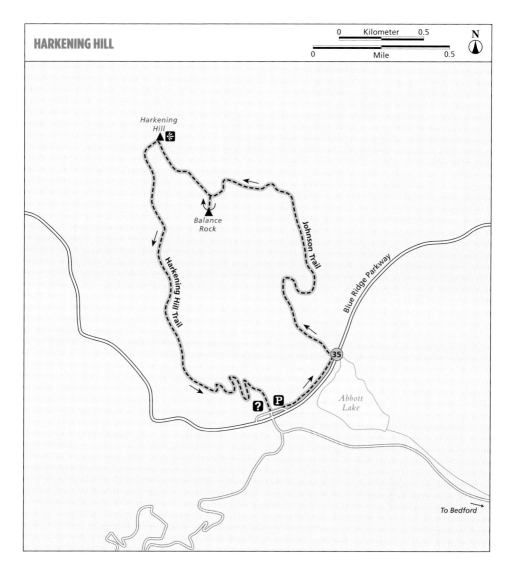

0   Kilometer   0.5

0   Mile   0.5

N

Harkening Hill

Balance Rock

Johnson Trail

Harkening Hill Trail

Blue Ridge Parkway

35

? P

Abbott Lake

To Bedford

a trail sign. Retrace your steps, then turn left on the Johnson Trail. In just 0.1 mile you will arrive at Harkening Hill. A large weathered sign lets you know that, yes, this is the place, you have reached the summit of Harkening Hill. Settle in on the rocky outcrop and revel in the north-facing views across the mountains. The panoramas are spectacular, especially in the fall.

From here, continue circling on the hiking trail. You'll see some more cool boulders and what appears to be a second "balance rock" (though there is no signage) at the 2.8-mile mark. The trail slowly descends and you'll encounter some easy switchbacks on the

◀ Top: A large trail sign greets visitors near the outdoor amphitheater at the Peaks of Otter Visitor Center

Bottom: There's more to this hike than summit views across the Blue Ridge Mountains. Follow a short spur trail less than 0.1 mile from the summit to see Balance Rock.

way down before exiting the trail at the 3.5-mile mark, just behind the visitor center's outdoor amphitheater. Simply walk around to the parking area and your loop hike is complete.

MILES AND DIRECTIONS

0.0   Begin at the east end of the parking area at the Peaks of Otter Visitor Center. Continue east on a small walking path.

0.3   Turn left at the trail sign for Harkening Hill.

0.8   Turn left at the trail sign for Balance Rock and Harkening Hill.

1.5   Turn left onto a short spur trail to Balance Rock. Retrace your steps, then turn left to reconnect with the Johnson Trail.

1.6   Arrive at Harkening Hill. Take in the views, then continue on the trail.

3.5   Exit the trail behind the visitor center's outdoor amphitheater. Walk around the building to the parking area. Your hike is complete.

OPTION

For a slightly longer hike—3.9 miles—that includes historic Johnson Farm, start at the east end of the visitor center parking area and follow the path for 0.3 mile. Bypass the first sign for Harkening Hill, then turn left at the second trail sign for the Johnson Farm Loop Trail. At the 1.1-mile mark, turn right at the sign for Harkening Hill and Balance Rock onto the Harkening Hill Trail. Then follow directions above to loop back around to the visitor center.

◀ Top: A weathered sign greets you at the top of Harkening Hill to let you know that, yes, you have reached the summit. This is the place.

Bottom: From the top of Harkening Hill, soak up all the spectacular views across the Blue Ridge Mountains. The vistas are especially beautiful in the fall.

36 MCAFEE KNOB

McAfee Knob, one of the most photographed spots on the entire Appalachian Trail, wows with sensational views of the Roanoke Valley, Catawba Valley, and North Mountain.

Start: Main parking area on Catawba Valley Drive
Elevation gain: 1,654 feet
Distance: 8.0 miles out and back
Difficulty: Moderate
Hiking time: 5 to 6 hours
Best season: Year-round
Fees and permits: Free
Trail contact: Appalachian National Scenic Trail, PO Box 50, Harpers Ferry, WV; (304) 535-6278; www.nps.gov/appa/
Dogs: Yes
Trail surface: Mostly dirt, sand, and rock trails, some gravel and wooden steps
Land status: Public land
Nearest town: Salem
Maps: National Geographic's Trails Illustrated Topographic Map 1504

(Appalachian Trail: Bailey Gap to Calf Mountain)
Amenities: Porta-potties
Maximum grade: 16%
Cell service: Reliable
Special considerations: There is alternative parking on Old Catawba Road, at the Catawba Sustainability Center and Catawba Community Center. Spur trails from both locations lead to the Appalachian Trail, but also tack on an extra 1.5 miles each way. A new (in 2022) shuttle takes hikers from the I-81 Exit 140 Park & Ride lot to the trailhead Mar through Nov. Tickets can be purchased online at https://mcafeeshuttle.com.

FINDING THE TRAILHEAD

The trailhead is located across Catawba Valley Drive from the main parking area (space for only a couple dozen cars). **GPS:** N37°22'49.2" / W80°05'25.0"

THE CLIMB

There's no question that McAfee Knob lays claim to more than a few superlatives, including the most photographed spot on the Appalachian Trail. The knob itself, which juts from the rocky outcrop, is instantly recognizable to many hikers. According to AllTrails, McAfee Knob is the second most popular hike in Virginia. It's also widely considered the favorite hike in the Virginia Triple Crown, a trifecta of Instagram-worthy hikes near Roanoke, which also includes Dragon's Tooth and Tinker Cliffs. Just look at the parking lot on any given Saturday at 7:30 a.m. Yes, 7:30 a.m. Cars parked everywhere. (Be forewarned: The local authorities are not hesitant to tow illegally parked vehicles.) It's a bucket-list hike for many hikers.

From the parking lot, *carefully* cross over to the sign that reads "To McAfee Knob." This is your starting point. There are two routes to McAfee Knob. You can hike the northbound Appalachian Trail all the way to the summit, or you can hop over to the

Top: The Catawba Mountain Shelter is one of two hikers' shelters that can ▶ be found along the Appalachian Trail on the way to McAfee Knob.

Bottom: Along the way, hikers encounter several guiding signs to help ensure they don't miss McAfee Knob, one of the most photographed spots on the Appalachian Trail.

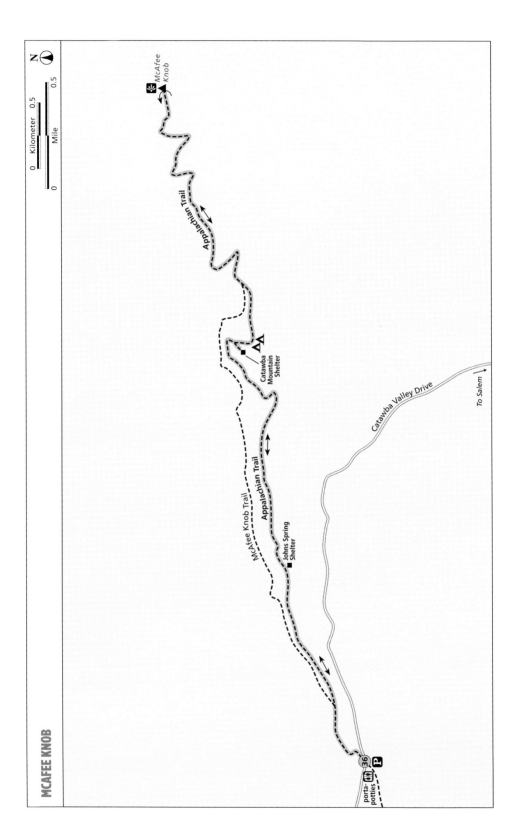

MCAFEE KNOB

McAfee Knob

Appalachian Trail

Catawba Mountain Shelter

McAfee Knob Trail

Appalachian Trail

Johns Spring Shelter

Catawba Valley Drive

To Salem

porta-potties

N

0   Kilometer   0.5

0   Mile   0.5

From protruding and often-photographed McAfee Knob, soak in 270-degree views of the Roanoke Valley, Catawba Valley, and North Mountain.

McAfee Knob Trail (a wide fire road) for 2.2 miles—between the 0.3-mile mark and the 2.5-mile mark. Since the latter is a wider stretch of hiking trail, it's a popular option for families with small children and those who want more space. Some find this path less interesting since there are no shelters to see along the way, but it all depends on what you are looking for from this hike.

For this hike, we'll guide you through the more popular of the two routes, on the Appalachian Trail. From the trailhead, enjoy a mild forested ascent, including wooden steps built into the trail, to a marker at the 0.3-mile mark, then veer right at the trail kiosk to stay on the northbound white-blazed Appalachian Trail. From here, the hiking trail narrows and undulates as it goes—a little up, a little down. You'll climb steps, then more steps, then even more steps. Thankfully, each set of steps includes no more than a dozen steps.

At the 1.0-mile mark, you'll reach a sign for the Johns Spring Shelter. It's a common lean-to hikers' shelter that you'll frequently see along the Appalachian Trail. It's just steps off the trail and has a picnic table, a fire pit, and a sprinkling of campsites for backpacking tents. Continue on the Appalachian Trail and you'll cross over a couple of easygoing creeks before arriving at the Catawba Mountain Shelter at the 2.2-mile mark. Given it's about 8 miles on average from one shelter to the next shelter, according to the Appalachian Trail Conservancy, it's quite unusual to see two hikers' shelters on such a short stretch of trail. Just past the Catawba Mountain Shelter, you'll also see a large campsite for backpackers to overnight while on the trail.

At the 2.5-mile mark, the McAfee Knob Trail merges with the Appalachian Trail. You'll then reach yet another set of wooden steps to ascend. From here, the trail steepens and narrows as you follow the white blazes up to McAfee Knob. You'll also encounter some rocks here and there, both large and small, but no ankle-twisting rock scrambles.

You'll reach a sign at the 4.0-mile mark that points you to the left for the overlook. If you were to miss this sign, you would continue on the Appalachian Trail, never to see McAfee Knob (at least, not today). Once you make the turn to the overlook, get ready to be bowled over by breathtaking 270-degree views across the Catawba Valley, Roanoke Valley, and North Mountain. So many people both talk about this hike and have it on their bucket list that it's good to know that this hike is absolutely "as advertised." But busy. It lives up to the hype, but you'll encounter a lot of other hikers at the top who also want to know whether this hike lives up to the hype. Thankfully, there's plenty of space to take a seat, though you may have to wait a bit to get a photo atop protruding McAfee Knob. That's okay. Just take your time and soak in all the views before you retrace your steps down the mountain. Note that at the 5.5-mile mark, you will again reach the McAfee Knob Trail. You can either turn right here to take that trail back to the parking area, or you can retrace your steps via the Appalachian Trail. Either way, your hike is complete at the 8.0-mile mark.

The author poses from the rocky outcrop atop McAfee Knob.

MILES AND DIRECTIONS

0.0 Begin at the trailhead for the Appalachian Trail across Catawba Valley Drive from the main parking area.

0.3 Veer right to stay on the Appalachian Trail.

1.0 Reach the Johns Spring Shelter.

2.2 Arrive at the Catawba Mountain Shelter, then a large campsite.

2.5 The McAfee Knob Trail merges with the Appalachian Trail. Continue straight ahead for the Appalachian Trail.

4.0 Turn left at the "Overlook" sign directing you to McAfee Knob. In a few more steps, take in all the views. Retrace your steps to the trailhead.

8.0 Arrive back at the trailhead. Your hike is complete.

37 PEARIS MOUNTAIN

This Appalachian Trail hike in Pearisburg includes two big vistas, Angel's Rest View Rock and Wilburn Valley Overlook. Both rocky viewpoints are wildly scenic and rewarding.

Start: Cross Avenue in Pearisburg
Elevation gain: 1,709 feet
Distance: 5.0 miles out and back
Difficulty: Strenuous
Hiking time: 3 to 4 hours
Best season: Year-round
Fees and permits: Free
Trail contact: Appalachian National Scenic Trail, PO Box 50, Harpers Ferry, WV; (304) 535-6278; www.nps.gov/appa/

Dogs: Yes
Trail surface: Mostly dirt and gravel trails, some stone steps
Land status: National scenic trail
Nearest town: Pearisburg
Maps: National Geographic Trails Illustrated Topographic Map 787 (Blacksburg, New River Valley)
Amenities: None
Maximum grade: 30% (stone steps)
Cell service: Reliable

FINDING THE TRAILHEAD

The trailhead is located on Cross Avenue. There is no designated parking area, but there's room for a half-dozen cars to park about 100 paces past the trailhead on Cross Avenue. **GPS:** N37°19'45.7" / W80°45'04.1"

THE CLIMB

There are many fantastic summit hikes that feature stretches along the Appalachian Trail, including this southbound hike to the rocky overlook atop Pearis Mountain (elevation 3,767 feet) in Pearisburg. On the way up—or on the way back—a second overlook called Angel's Rest View Rock stuns hikers with bird's-eye views across this small town in Southwest Virginia.

The climb begins at the trailhead on Cross Avenue, about 1 mile or so away from Main Street, a Dairy Queen, a Hardee's, a Food Lion, and a hikers' hostel called Angel's Rest Hiker's Haven. As you can imagine, this area is a popular stopover for hungry and weary Appalachian Trail thru-hikers. The only downside is that it's an uphill climb back to the long-distance trail.

At the trailhead, six or seven steps boost hikers up onto the Appalachian Trail from the road. The climb begins now, friends. Thankfully, more than a dozen switchbacks, as well as built-in stone steps, on this stretch of trail make the hike less ruthless. Always a plus. In spring, cheery purple phlox lines both sides of the trail, making the ascent even more manageable.

At the 0.6-mile mark, there's a large rock that is well suited as a bench. Take a seat, and a deep breath, as you will have already climbed 450 feet in elevation at this point. As you continue on, there is a mini rock scramble at the 1.5-mile mark. Watch your footing. At the 1.8-mile mark, you'll arrive at a mini maze of massive boulders, as well as a sign beckoning hikers to turn right for Angel's Rest View Rock. From here, it's a very short walk to a boulder that's just right for angels—or hikers—to stand watch over the New River and Pearisburg down below.

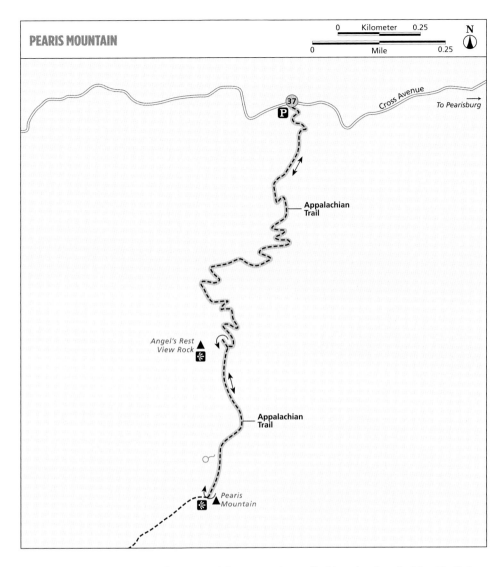

Kilometer

Mile

N

37

P

Cross Avenue

To Parisburg

Appalachian
Trail

Angel's Rest
View Rock

Appalachian
Trail

Pearis
Mountain

Retrace your steps, then turn right to continue climbing the Appalachian Trail. In a few steps you'll reach a primitive campsite with a fire ring on the right. Keep climbing; you're almost there. But first, a blue-blazed spur trail that leads to a spring turns up at the 2.3-mile mark. You'll reach a heavenly overlook at the 2.5-mile mark for incredible views across the Wilburn Valley. Sit and stay awhile because the views are beyond incredible. Once you've soaked it all in, retrace your steps to the parking area. Your hike is complete at the 5.0-mile mark.

◀ Top: More than a dozen switchbacks and stone steps built into the trail make the challenging climb to the Wilburn Valley Overlook manageable.

Bottom: The far-reaching views from the Wilburn Valley Overlook are outstanding, worth every ounce of your efforts to reach the rocky outcrop.

A short spur trail leads to Angel's Rest View Rock, which is just right for angels and hikers to keep watch over the New River and the town of Pearisburg.

MILES AND DIRECTIONS

0.0 Begin at the trailhead on Cross Avenue. Be sure to take the southbound stretch of the Appalachian Trail that goes up the hill.

1.8 Turn right at the trail sign for Angel's Rest View Rock. Retrace your steps to the Appalachian Trail.

At the 1.8-mile mark, turn right at the trail sign for the short walk to enjoy big views from Angel's Rest View Rock.

1.9   Turn right to continue south on the Appalachian Trail.

2.3   Reach a blue-blazed spur trail that leads to a spring.

2.5   Arrive at the Wilburn Valley Overlook atop Pearis Mountain. Retrace your steps to the parking area.

5.0   Arrive back at the parking area. Your hike is complete.

38 SHARP TOP

A rugged hike along the Sharp Top Trail in Bedford leads visitors to 360-degree views from atop the most popular of Virginia's three Peaks of Otter mountains.

Start: Sharp Top Store
Elevation gain: 1,253 feet
Distance: 3.3 miles out and back
Difficulty: Strenuous
Hiking time: 2.5 to 3.5 hours
Best season: Year-round
Fees and permits: Free
Trail contact: Peaks of Otter Visitor Center, 85919 Blue Ridge Parkway, Bedford; (540) 586-4496; www.nps.gov/blri/
Dogs: Yes
Trail surface: Mostly dirt and rock trails, some stone steps
Land status: National park (Blue Ridge Parkway)

Nearest town: Bedford
Maps: National Geographic Trails Illustrated Topographic Map 789 (Lexington, Blue Ridge Mountains)
Amenities: Flush toilets, picnic tables, visitor center, campground, camp store
Maximum grade: 29% (stairs)
Cell service: Spotty
Special considerations: A seasonal shuttle is available that takes visitors to within 0.25 mile of the summit. Day-of-departure tickets can be purchased at the Sharp Top Store in the parking lot.

FINDING THE TRAILHEAD

The trailhead is located to the left of the Sharp Top Store, across the Blue Ridge Parkway from the Peaks of Otter Visitor Center at milepost 85.6. The parking lot can hold at least two dozen cars. However, on peak hiking days, like fall weekends, it fills quickly and can be overflowing by 10 a.m.—arrive early.
GPS: N37°26'36.2" / W79°36'34.4"

THE CLIMB

Bedford is best known for two primary attractions: the National D-Day Memorial and the Peaks of Otter, three hikeable mountains that reward tenacious hikers with wildly spectacular views across the Blue Ridge Mountains. Of the three peaks, Sharp Top is easily the most popular, boasting 360-degree views across the Jefferson National Forest from atop this 3,875-foot-tall mountain. It also helps that a seasonal shuttle service is available to transport hike-reluctant visitors to within 1,500 feet of the summit, making Sharp Top the most accessible of the three mountain peaks, too.

The Sharp Top Store is a small camp store that sells supplies, T-shirts, and snacks, as well as shuttle tickets for the more leisurely journey to the top. An outdoor patio behind the camp store tempts hikers to settle in and stay for a while after their summit hike.

As you prepare to take your first steps, note the educational placards on either side of the trailhead, which tell of the popularity of Sharp Top that goes well beyond present-day visitors. In fact, more than 8,000 years ago, Indigenous peoples were drawn to Sharp

Top: The curiously pointed Sharp Top is one of three Peaks of ▶ Otter mountains on the Blue Ridge Parkway near Bedford.

Bottom: Read the placards at the trailhead before taking your first steps to learn more about Sharp Top Mountain.

A stone shelter at the top of Sharp Top Mountain once served as a restaurant in the 1950s and 1960s.

Top, presumably for its curiously pointed top and rugged terrain that rises so precipitously from the earth.

The hike begins with a dozen stone steps before reaching a path that leads off to the left to the Peaks of Otter Campground, a 141-site campground that sits adjacent to 24-acre Abbott Lake. This campground is open seasonally from late May to late October. Walk past this side path to stay on the Sharp Top Trail, which becomes mostly a dirt path at this point. At the 0.2-mile mark, the trail crosses over the road used by the shuttle to take visitors to the top. From here, the hiking trail alternates several times between dirt trail and stone steps, at times with handrails.

Get ready for a change of scenery at the 1.0-mile mark when gigantic boulders begin to materialize on either side of the Sharp Top Trail. These were formed over many years by weather-related decomposition and breaking up of the diorite rock that makes up the mountain. You'll see more massive, and seemingly out of place, boulders once you reach the summit, too.

In a few more steps, at the 1.2-mile mark, you will approach a trail sign and have a decision to make. You can turn right to reach Buzzard's Roost in 600 feet or you can turn left to continue on 1,900 feet to Sharp Top. For this hike, we'll go to Sharp Top first, and then check out the views from Buzzard's Roost on the way back down the mountain.

As you continue on the Sharp Top Trail, you'll note spur trails on either side of the main trail at the 1.5-mile mark. These are the trails that lead up from the shuttle bus stop for the final ascent to the summit of Sharp Top. You will arrive at the top of Sharp

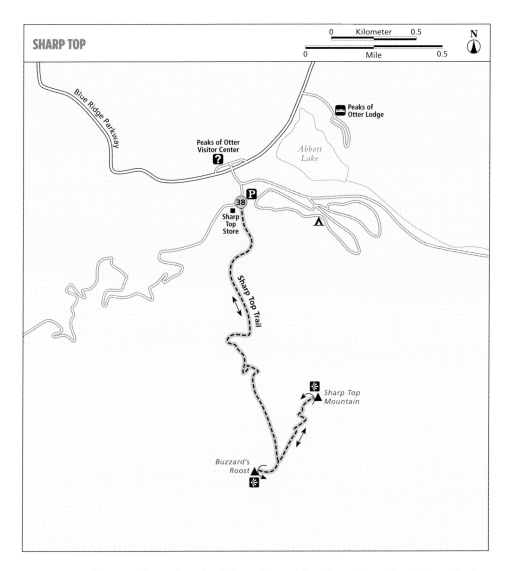

Top at the 1.6-mile mark and will be welcomed by a large Sharp Top Mountain sign apprising visitors that Sharp Top was once thought to be the highest peak in Virginia. Years later, surveyors found this not to be the case. Interestingly, one of the other Peaks of Otter, Flat Top, is taller than Sharp Top at an elevation of 4,001 feet. Still, it's stone from Sharp Top that can be found inside the Washington Monument in Washington, DC, to honor founding father George Washington. An inscription reads: "From Otter's summit, Virginia's loftiest peak, to crown a monument to Virginia's noblest son."

You'll quickly notice that Sharp Top does not have a rugged, craggy summit like you would find at Humpback Rocks or Mount Pleasant. Instead, you'll find stone terraces, walkways and steps, even a stone shelter, which was once used as a restaurant in the 1950s and 1960s (guests arrived by way of mule-drawn carriages). Take time to walk around, reveling in 360-degree views across the Blue Ridge Mountains. It's no surprise that with

such views this is a coveted mountaintop destination for savoring colorful sunrises and sunsets.

Take in all the views, then retrace your steps to the base of Sharp Top. But first, take the side trail to Buzzard's Roost at the 1.9-mile mark. There is a massive rock to scramble up for the very best west-facing views, but it's no cakewalk to reach the top. The vistas also aren't nearly as good as they are from Sharp Top. However, this less-trafficked viewpoint is worth a quick stopover on the return hike to the parking area. Your hike is complete at the 3.3-mile mark.

MILES AND DIRECTIONS

0.0 Begin at the trailhead to the left of the Sharp Top Store. Stop to read the educational placards, then walk up the stone steps. Continue walking past the side trail for the campground.

0.2 Cross over the road used by the shuttle service to reach the summit of Sharp Top.

1.2 Arrive at an intersection. Turn left to continue on the Sharp Top Trail.

1.6 Reach the summit of Sharp Top Mountain. Retrace your steps.

1.9 Arrive at an intersection. Stay left to walk out to the Buzzard's Roost overlook. Retrace your steps to the intersection.

2.1 Turn left to continue descending on the Sharp Top Trail.

3.3 Arrive back at the trailhead. Your hike is complete.

This Appalachian Trail hike begins with a leg-stretching 3-mile warm-up and a stopover at a hikers' shelter on the way up to big mountain vistas from high atop Sugar Run Mountain.

Start: Parking area on US Forestry Road
Elevation gain: 2,008 feet
Distance: 10.8-mile loop
Difficulty: Strenuous
Hiking time: 5.5 to 6.5 hours
Best season: Year-round
Fees and permits: Free
Trail contact: George Washington and Jefferson National Forest (Eastern Divide Ranger District), 110 Southpark Dr., Blacksburg; (540)
552-4641; www.fs.usda.gov/detail/gwj
Dogs: Yes
Trail surface: Mostly dirt and rock trails
Land status: National forest
Nearest town: Pearisburg
Maps: National Geographic's Trails Illustrated Topographic Map 787 (Blacksburg, New River Valley)
Amenities: None
Maximum grade: 24%
Cell service: Reliable

FINDING THE TRAILHEAD

The trailhead is located in the northeast corner of a small parking lot on US Forestry Road. **GPS:** N37°13'02.1" / W80°51'40.3"

THE CLIMB

There's a lot to love about this hike in the Jefferson National Forest to big views atop Sugar Run Mountain (elevation 4,062 feet) near Pearisburg, but only if you do it right. As in, counterclockwise. That direction starts off this 10-plus-miler with a leg-stretching 3.0-mile walk through the woods. Once the climb really kicks in, after you pass the hikers' shelter, you'll be thankful for this warm-up.

From the trailhead, look for the blue blazes that will lead you through dense rhododendron thickets to the Ribble Trail. There are no signs, but get ready to cross over Dismal Creek and trust that you're going in the right direction. Just keep your eyes open for the next blue blaze. At the 0.6-mile mark, turn left onto a northbound stretch of the Appalachian Trail when you see the sign that's nailed to a tree (at last, a sign). From here, you will flit back and forth between sections of mixed forest and dense rhododendron tunnels (or, simply, "rhodey tunnels") that seem to block out all light at some points. You'll also traverse at least nine small wooden footbridges.

It can be easy to hike at a rapid clip when the trail is flat and wide, but don't move too quickly or you may glide right past a beautiful high-elevation pond (that's also green in color). At the 2.4-mile mark, a short but steep spur trail leads up to this breathtaking pond. You can see a couple of campsites on the opposite side of the pond. Retrace your steps, then continue on the Appalachian Trail, though in a few more steps you'll be adjacent to the pond again. Yes, you don't need to hike up the spur trail, but the better views are definitely there, along the pond's southwest edge.

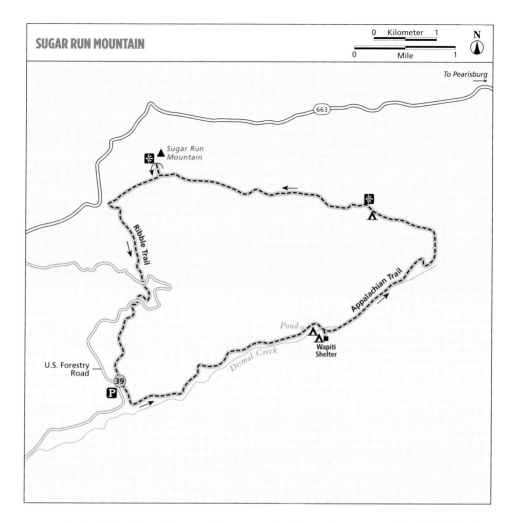

SUGAR RUN MOUNTAIN

Sugar Run
Mountain

Ribble Trail

Appalachian Trail

Pond

Wapiti
Shelter

Dismal Creek

U.S. Forestry
Road

39

663

To Pearisburg

At the 2.8-mile mark, turn right to wander along a short spur trail to Wapiti Shelter, a typical lean-to that's a common shelter style along the Appalachian Trail. There is a picnic table and a fire ring, as well as lots of open spaces for tents. Plan to stop here to rehydrate, eat lunch, or simply collect yourself before you continue on, because this next section is strenuous. It starts out gradual, but then each step will further challenge you. But first, you will cross over Dismal Creek at the 3.4-mile mark. The refreshing cascades are like the calm before the storm.

The grade increases at the 3.5-mile mark. Okay, let's do this. You will want to take many breaks on this heart-pounding stretch of the Appalachian Trail. A primitive camp-site comes into view at the 5.2-mile mark. This is a good spot to rehydrate and catch your breath. In a few more steps, at the 5.4-mile mark, look for a small rocky outcrop with nice views. This is another good spot to take a short break.

◄ Top: On the way to the top of Sugar Run Mountain, you'll cross over at least nine wooden footbridges in a mix of deciduous forest and dense tunnels of rhododendron thickets.
Bottom: At the 2.4-mile mark is a pleasant surprise: A breathtaking high-elevation pond greets hikers on their way north and south along the Appalachian Trail.

At the 7.6-mile mark, you're so close you can taste it (yes, 4.0 miles later), but pay attention or you may miss the rocky overlook. An unmarked spur trail leads off to the right while the Appalachian Trail continues to the left (look for the white blaze on a fallen log). Stay to the right. It's only 0.1 mile to the overlook. You'll pass several radio towers on the way, as well as a large stone fire pit that is steps from the overlook. Get ready: The northeast-facing views across the Wilburn Valley are simply sensational.

Once you've taken it all in, retrace your steps on the spur trail and turn right onto the Appalachian Trail. Your time on the Appalachian Trail ends at the 8.5-mile mark. You'll see a sign for the blue-blazed Ribble Trail. Turn left here to slowly begin your descent to the parking area. The trail is steep, narrow, and covered with leaves. It even feels like a ditch at some points, making it more challenging to descend on (though it may have been worse to climb). You'll cross over a gravel road twice before you approach a beaver dam at the 9.9-mile mark. The end is near as the trail flattens, then you're back in the parking area. Your hike is complete at the 10.8-mile mark. Celebrate, maybe with a splash at Dismal Falls, which is an easy 10-minute drive north of the trailhead for this hike.

MILES AND DIRECTIONS

0.0 Begin on a blue-blazed connector trail in the northeast corner of the parking lot.

0.6 Turn left onto the white-blazed Appalachian Trail.

2.4 A short spur trail leads to a small green pond with campsites. Retrace your steps.

2.8 Turn right for the Wapiti Shelter. Retrace your steps to the Appalachian Trail.

3.4 Cross over Dismal Creek.

5.4 Reach a rocky overlook with scenic mountain vistas.

7.6 Turn right onto an unmarked spur trail to reach the overlook.

7.7 Arrive at the rocky outcrop atop Sugar Run Mountain. Retrace your steps.

7.8 Turn right onto the Appalachian Trail.

8.5 Turn left onto the blue-blazed Ribble Trail.

10.8 Arrive back at the parking area. Your hike is complete.

Top: Stop for lunch or hydration at the Wapiti Shelter, which turns up at ▶ the 2.8-mile mark. This is your last stop before the climb really begins.

Bottom: Soak up all the views across the Wilburn Valley from the rocky outcrop atop Sugar Run Mountain. You are worthy.

The hike to Tinker Cliffs and Tinker Mountain boasts multiple rocky outcrops for soaking up all the views across the Catawba Valley near Roanoke.

Start: Parking area for Andy Layne Trail
Elevation gain: 1,995 feet
Distance: 8.1 miles out and back
Difficulty: Moderate
Hiking time: 4.5 to 6 hours
Best season: Year-round
Fees and permits: Free
Trail contact: Appalachian National Scenic Trail, PO Box 50, Harpers Ferry, WV; (304) 535-6278; www.nps.gov/appa/

Dogs: Yes
Trail surface: Mostly dirt and rock trails
Land status: Public land
Nearest town: Salem
Maps: National Geographic's Trails Illustrated Topographic Map 1504 (Appalachian Trail: Bailey Gap to Calf Mountain)
Amenities: None
Maximum grade: 19%
Cell service: Reliable

FINDING THE TRAILHEAD

The trailhead is located on Catawba Road, at the parking area for the Andy Layne Trail. There's room for a couple dozen cars, but it can be a tight squeeze. Your best bet is to arrive early, especially on fair-weather weekends.
GPS: N37°27'27.2" / W80°01'02.3"

THE CLIMB

The hike to Tinker Cliffs on Tinker Mountain is one hike in Virginia's Triple Crown trifecta of hikes near Roanoke, which includes McAfee Knob, Dragon's Tooth, and Tinker Cliffs. It's also the most underrated of the three summit hikes.

The blue-blazed Andy Layne Trail begins at the extra-large trail kiosk at the trailhead. There's a Tinker Cliffs Area Map, as well as trail rules and resources, like shuttle services and leave no trace principles. The first 3.0 miles of this hike are on private property, so stay on the trail, though this is a good rule regardless of the trail and land status. In fact, the private land was donated by the next-door Roanoke Cement Company. That noted, you're likely to hear rumblings from the cement plant every now and again.

Interestingly, this summit hike kicks off with a descent. At the 0.2-mile mark, get ready to go down more than four dozen steps, but don't worry, you'll make up those steps and plenty more. But first, at the 0.6-mile mark, you'll cross over a footbridge that guides you over flowing Little Catawba Creek, followed by a wide-open clearing and a second footbridge, this time over Catawba Creek. Keep your eyes open for cows, which often cool themselves in the refreshing creeks.

Your ascent begins around the 0.9-mile mark as you climb a handful of steps, but then it's pretty calm, a simple walk in the woods. The steps return at the 1.7-mile mark. I hope you're ready. Climb more than one hundred wooden steps, then take a breath and tackle another sixty or so steps. That's pretty much all the steps. Phew.

◀ Early in the hike, a wooden footbridge guides hikers over gently flowing Catawba Creek.

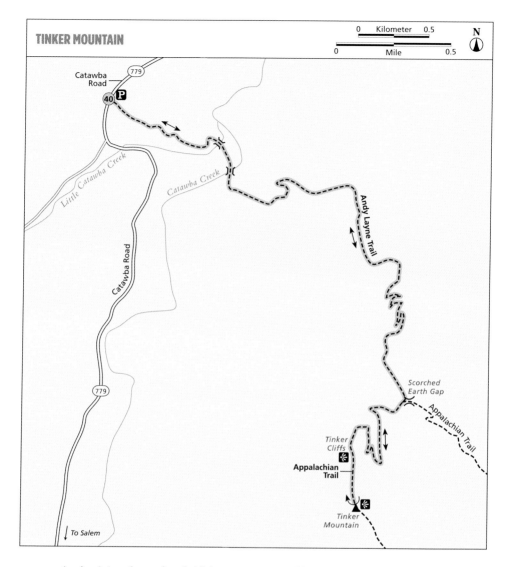

0   Kilometer   0.5

0   Mile   0.5

N

Catawba Road

779

P

40

Little Catawba Creek

Catawba Creek

Catawba Road

Andy Layne Trail

779

Scorched Earth Gap

Appalachian Trail

Tinker Cliffs

Appalachian Trail

Tinker Mountain

To Salem

At the 2.1-mile mark, a half-dozen or so switchbacks manage your ascent up Tinker Mountain. You'll then arrive at the Appalachian Trail at the 3.0-mile mark, at a junction called Scorched Earth Gap. Turn right to head southbound on the white-blazed Appalachian Trail and you'll begin ascending a ridgeline to Tinker Cliffs.

The bottom of the cliffs come into view—as in, alongside the trail—at the 3.5-mile mark. At this point, you're getting close, but there's still more trail to climb. In a few more steps, you'll see rocky outcrops with partially obstructed vistas. No need to jockey for views. Wide-open panoramas across the Catawba Valley are just a few more steps up the Appalachian Trail.

◀ Top: Get ready for dozens and dozens of wooden steps that guide your ascent along the blue-blazed Andy Layne Trail.

Bottom: There are so many rocky outcrops at the top of Tinker Mountain. There's plenty of room for everyone to sit and soak in the spectacular views.

The views across the Catawba Valley are magical. You'll want to take in all the panoramas before making the return trek to the parking area.

At the 3.8-mile mark, you will reach Tinker Cliffs. There is a large rocky outcrop with far-reaching views. If this overlook is crowded, continue on. There are so many overlooks boasting booming vistas. In fact, big views and rocky outcrops continue for at least 0.2 mile, to and past the summit for Tinker Mountain. Once you've seen it all, retrace your steps to the parking area. Your hike is complete at the 8.1-mile mark.

MILES AND DIRECTIONS

0.0 Begin at the large trail kiosk at the parking area.

0.6 Cross a wooden footbridge over Little Catawba Creek.

0.7 Cross a wooden footbridge over Catawba Creek.

3.0 Turn right onto the Appalachian Trail (southbound).

3.8 Arrive at Tinker Cliffs. Continue on to Tinker Mountain.

4.05 Reach the summit of Tinker Mountain. Retrace your steps to the parking area.

8.1 Arrive back at the parking area. Your hike is complete.

APPENDIX A:
FOR MORE INFORMATION

The following are excellent sources of information on many of the trails, parks, recreation areas, and campgrounds referenced in this book.

Appalachian Trail Conservancy
799 Washington St., PO Box 807
Harpers Ferry, WV 25425
(304) 535-6331
https://appalachiantrail.org

Blue Ridge Parkway Association
PO Box 2136
Asheville, NC 28802
(828) 670-1924
www.blueridgeparkway.org

Shenandoah National Park Headquarters
3655 US 211 E.
Luray, VA 22835
(540) 999-3500 (for non-emergencies)
(800) 732-0911 (for park emergencies)
www.nps.gov/shen/

Shenandoah National Park Association
3655 US 211 E.
Luray, VA 22835
(540) 999-3582
https://snpbooks.org

Virginia Department of Conservation and Recreation (Virginia State Parks)
600 E. Main St., 24th Floor
Richmond, VA 23219
(800) 933-7275
www.dcr.virginia.gov/state-parks

US Department of Agriculture (George Washington and Jefferson National Forests)
5162 Valleypointe Parkway (forest supervisor's office)
Roanoke, VA 24019
(540) 265-5100
www.fs.usda.gov/gwj

Park maps can often be found on-site at state, national, and regional parks as well as online for download before arriving at a trailhead. Alternatively, National Geographic creates a variety of its Trails Illustrated topographic maps.

National Geographic Maps
212 Beaver Brook Canyon Rd.
Evergreen, CO 80439
(800) 962-1643
www.natgeomaps.com

APPENDIX B: FURTHER READING

The following books were helpful in the creation of this guidebook:

Gildart, Bert and Jane. *Hiking Shenandoah National Park*. FalconGuides, 2022.

Johnson, Randy. *Hiking the Blue Ridge Parkway*. FalconGuides, 2022.

The following online resources are also valuable in identifying and researching hiking trails:

AllTrails.com

HikingUpward.com

HikingProject.com

HIKE INDEX